Love Lessons
from
Bad Breakups

Love Lessons from Bad Breakups

Sherry Amatenstein

A Perigee Book

A Perigee Book
Published by The Berkley Publishing Group
A division of Penguin Putnam Inc.
375 Hudson Street
New York, New York 10014

Copyright © 2002 by Sherry Amatenstein
Book design by Tiffany Kukec
Cover design by Charles Björklund
Cover art by Artville /Mona Daly

First edition: January 2002

Published simultaneously in Canada.

Visit our website at www.penguinputnam.com

Library of Congress Cataloging-in-Publication Data
Amatenstein, Sherry.
    Love lessons from bad breakups / Sherry Amatenstein.—1st ed.
        p.   cm.
    Includes bibliographical references.
    ISBN 0-399-52741-9
        I. Man-woman relationships. 2. Separation (Psychology)
3. Couples. 4. Love. 5. Intimacy (Psychology) I. Title

HQ801 .A5293 2002
306.7—dc21
                                                    2001036670

Printed in the United States of America

10   9   8   7   6   5   4   3   2   1

Dedication

To my biological family: I got so lucky when I was born into the Amatenstein clan. You are the dearest people on earth to me. You may not always understand why I do the things I do, but you love me regardless.

To the family of my heart whom I've created over the years—a fabulous band of people who have reveled in my joys and nursed me through my heartbreaks.

Finally, to **my** exes, who taught me so much about the nature of love, loss, and the regeneration of the heart and spirit. I'm grateful to all of you.

Contents

Acknowledgments

First, a heartfelt thank you to my agent, Linda Konner, who led me to the second person I want to thank—my editor, Sheila Curry Oakes. Thank you, Sheila, for your faith, support and granting of an extension to my deadline!

I'd also like to thank Eileen, Charity, and the rest of the crew at iVillage. I'm so glad to be part of the team.

Next I want to thank Robin Westen—the only person who saw any of the manuscript in progress. She fired me up to go on and write the next eighteen chapters!

I'd also like to thank Laura Day—great intuitive, even greater friend for her unswerving faith in me and support of this project.

Next, I offer up a special thank-you to Irina Harris, who helped me realize that "my exes" stories were about so much more than passion gone wrong.

To David La Barca, who more than once laughed away my fears that I'd never be able to "do justice to my exes."

I'd be remiss not to thank anyone and everyone who gave me leads in the seemingly impossible quest to find sets of exes who would both be willing to talk to me.

My biggest thank-you goes of course to everyone whose story you will find in this book. These people gave generously of their time and spirit. They opened their veins and allowed me to bear witness to wounds that were still open. These brave souls candidly admitted their mistakes, shared their vulnerabilities, insights, and lessons learned.

Introduction

We've all read relationship books based on the romantic secrets of successful couples. They're crammed with tips like: *Communicate with each other; Don't go to bed angry; Give each other space when necessary.* This is valuable advice, but it doesn't cover the whole story. People eager for lasting love can glean information from an unexpected source—failed relationships. That is where this book comes in. *Love Lessons from Bad Breakups* is based on the mistakes of couples who didn't make it to happily ever after. Do as they didn't (and don't do as they did) and you might soon be choosing and engraving your wedding bands.

The format of *Love Lessons from Bad Breakups* is deceptively simple and entertaining yet *extremely* effective. Each chapter or love lesson is presented in three-part disharmony: *his, hers, and the truth.* Thus, while each presents negative examples of couples who didn't make it, reading them will leave you with hard-won but very positive love lessons.

The names of the men and women involved in these twenty-one tales of heartbreak have been changed to preserve their anonymity. Speaking from hindsight, they bravely and honestly relive their roller-coaster romances. The ex-couples' accounts, presented in their own words, are occasionally one-sided, accusatory, and jarringly disparate. In these instances I offer the pair a chance to respond to the other's charges, in a section called *Punch/Counterpunch*. Each chapter ends with my summary and analysis of the mistakes made by the former couple, what each should have done, could have done, and what *you* can do to avoid ramming your head smack into this particular romantic wall.

This book does not deal with relationships where there is serious physical and/or emotional abuse. The best solution in those cases is for the partners to seek professional help.

The aim here is not to cast one side as the villain and the other as victim. In some love lessons the partner primarily at fault is the male; in other lessons, the female; in still others, both are responsible for the dissolution of the relationship. I believe in equal-fault breakups.

Just as eyewitness accounts of a road accident invariably differ, the same holds true for a romantic wreck. In the latter case there is much value to be gleaned from examining the points of view of both sides—where their versions merge and where they differ.

Common patterns that emerged from my interviews from both halves of these split couples included a lack of similar values and goals, lack of commitment to the relationship, miscommunication (the gulf between man-and-woman-speak looms ever large) and fear. It's a fear of losing oneself in the other, of fully trusting, then being abandoned that catapults each partner into running from rather than toward each other. The subconscious thinking goes: "I'll mistreat you before you can mistreat me."

Not every couple will stay together if they avoid the patterns and pitfalls outlined in the following pages—or not every couple *should* stay together. But having knowledge, a foreshadowing of how certain actions you and/or your partner might take can precipitate certain outcomes, can help put you in control of the relationship . . . at least your part in it.

Just because a relationship ultimately ends doesn't mean it failed. If you are truly willing to examine where and why things went wrong, a breakup is a powerful teacher that can help better prepare you for the next opportunity at love.

And let's face it: Some relationships are meant to be, while some are meant to be avoided. These love lessons can help you avoid the latter.

Brian & Katy

Relationship b: 1995; d: 1998

Chapter 1

Cut the Cord Rather Than Breaking Up to Make up Again and Again and Again

Brian Says

Katy and I were together exclusively for a year and a half, then had a long, painful breakup. I kept trying to do it cleanly but I didn't know how.

I have two sisters and was raised to treat women with a lot of respect. In high school I got into my first relationship. It was quite destructive. My girlfriend was Brazilian and Italian, very emotional. I'd never seen my parents fight and here I was doing it twice hourly. Tina thought if she didn't get a rise out of me, something was wrong. She really got a rise when she had sex with a friend of mine.

After Tina, I vowed to be careful with my heart. No more going out on a limb and saying *I love you* when I could wind up later deciding I'd misjudged my feelings. That seemed like it would be disrespectful to the girl.

Then I met Katy and we got a flirtation going. But she had a boyfriend. Finally I said, "Kid, I like you but I don't want to be dicked around. I'll give you two weeks. If you call me, great. If not, I'm done." She called two weeks to the day.

Things got a little serious my sophomore year. I'd sleep over with her every once in awhile. We were both very social. Occasionally we'd have dinner alone but for the most part we'd hang out with our group of friends. We had a month-long breakup at one point but things quickly got back to normal.

In some ways my relationship with Katy was like an extracurricular project. I wanted to see if I could develop relationship-building skills. I guess it didn't help that I could never call her *girlfriend*. She was a nice kid, kind of cute. It wasn't until after we broke up that I realized I loved her. But I never loved her *enough*.

I was in a five-year pre-med program and school was very hard. Katy was really the best thing going on. I tried to be a good boyfriend. That meant that she never paid for a meal once the entire time we were together. It also meant that I tried to say *yes* to her as much as humanly possible, and that I tried to understand her gripes.

She took all these classes on interpersonal relationships and read *Cosmo* voraciously. She'd clip articles and quizzes for me to check out. It was really cute. We learned from our reading that it wasn't healthy to spring complaints on the other person. So I'd say to Katy, "Can we schedule time to discuss a grievance?" And I stopped shouting, "Shut up!" when I was angry. It was rude to be that crass with someone you cared about.

But I was adamant that when she graduated I wasn't going to play the long-distance game. We'd be through.

Katy kept talking about making a commitment. She also talked about converting to Judaism because she knew I couldn't marry out of my faith.

I considered her offer. A lot went into my decision to end

things on her graduation day. When it actually happened, I didn't know whether she believed it was over. She got in her car and had that smile-even-though-your-heart-is-breaking expression.

My plan was a clean break but a few weeks later we started talking. She came to visit me at school a couple of times. Every time we'd be together I'd say, "You're welcome to come to visit and we can have sex but that doesn't mean we're a couple again."

I knew she was nuts about me so I tried not to be fuzzy about my intentions. But it was a tricky situation. I'd say, "You're amazing but it's not going to work out." Katy had selective hearing and just heard, "You're amazing."

She'd ask, "Do we have a chance?" How do you answer that question? I wanted to say: "Never." Or, "If I'm thirty-six and I haven't met anyone as cool as you." Or: "It's not like I can't be happy with you but I think I can do better." That would be cruel so I'd say: "Possibly." And she'd grab on to that. Although there was some truth to "possibly," I probably shouldn't have said that word.

This on-again/off-again pattern continued when I started taking six-week internships in different locations. Katy and I had a couple of good times together. Then, in 1998 I was in San Francisco and she visited me for ten days. My invitation had been: "I have an apartment. You can stay here and see the city." She took it as: "You can come here and be with me."

She got pissed at me for not being totally attentive to her at a bar and wound up flirting with every guy in the place. Katy even gave out my telephone number to a few persistent callers who left messages for her on my machine long after she'd gone back to Michigan.

I wasn't jealous about this but it eased my guilt toward Katy. I'd been feeling bad that she loved me so much more than I loved her. After San Francisco I didn't feel I owed her anything.

On one hand, maybe I shouldn't have been in a relationship

with Katy, since I didn't dig her enough to ever propose. On the other hand, I was just twenty years old. I wanted to try a long-term relationship. And it was very rewarding. I just should have stuck to our first breakup—or our second or our third. I gave Katy a lot of mixed messages. It was selfish—I enjoyed having sex with her.

Now that she's dating someone we're finally true friends. In a perfect world, if I break up with my current girlfriend I'll try to make sure that my words and actions match.

Katy Says

Brian and I met at a Halloween party during my junior year at college. He wore a doctor's uniform and I was Minnie Mouse. I didn't think twice about him because I was still involved with Tim, my on-again/off-again boyfriend of three years. That relationship was totally bad; Tim wasn't good to me. But he was my first love so I couldn't let go.

Through all this Brian, who was a sophomore, kept asking me out. I finally said, "Oh *alright!*" We had a nice time but I still considered him as a friend. When he gave me a Christmas present, I thought, *"Oh no, now I have to buy him something."*

One day he announced, "I'm giving you two weeks. If I don't hear from you, it's over." I was like, "Fine." I didn't call; didn't miss him. Out of the blue it hit me. Brian was such a good person. He'd always treated me like gold.

I called. He said, "We can date but you first have to break up with your boyfriend." I did. We had sex, and from then on I was totally about Brian.

He seemed totally about me but he couldn't say *girlfriend.* Then, five months into the relationship I copped to totally loving him. He couldn't say the words back. This made me bothered . . . *very* bothered. Five months later the religion thing started cropping up. The weekend after I had brought him to a cousin's wedding he got invited to a family bar mitzvah. When I asked if he wanted me to go too, he said no. His parents wouldn't understand his dating a Catholic girl.

I called my mom and asked if I should be mad at Brian. She talked to a few people about the Jewish religion and found out they were strict about intermarriage. She said, "Katy, it will probably never work out."

I was devastated. Brian and I had been together nearly a year, he couldn't say I *love you*, and now this.

When he got back on campus Sunday night, I said, "I talked to my mom and if you can never get serious about me we have to break up." I gave him back his toothbrush. He broke it in half but didn't deny that religion mattered.

I left, but was totally sad. I broke out in a weird neck rash from the stress. I looked so gross I had to walk around in turtlenecks—and it was a balmy October.

Occasionally I'd run into Brian on campus. He seemed fine. I was so nonfunctional I went to the counseling center at school. The shrink wanted to talk about my childhood. This made me mad. I only wanted to talk about Brian.

I bumped into Brian again and asked if we could go back to his place and talk. I didn't drink anything but I felt drugged. We wound up having sex.

A few days later a friend of mine was in Brian's dorm. She overheard him asking his roommate for a condom so he could have sex with this girl.

This made me so angry that I took the mini refrigerator he'd given me for my room, taped condoms all over it along with a note, THE NEXT TIME YOU WANT TO HAVE SEX WITH THAT———BITCH, YOU'LL BE PREPARED and wheeled it outside my room. I called his friends and said Brian better come get the refrigerator or dogs would pee all over it.

When I came back from grocery shopping the refrigerator was

gone. My room was a mess. Brian's friends had blown up the condoms, smeared them with Vaseline and hung them over everything, including the doorknobs. I was mad, but it was also very funny.

A couple of days later after seeing Brian with a girl, I hung out with another guy, took some pills, and had sex. Brian found out, and the next time we ran into each other he said, "My heart is broken." I said mine was too. I didn't care about the religion thing anymore. In mid-November, after six weeks apart, Brian and I got back together.

It was like in those cheesy songs and stupid movies: Instantly my neck rash went away. Instantly I was totally happy. I thought all those corny things you think when you're crazy in love. It almost didn't bother me that Brian still wasn't saying "I love you." I'd get these lame excuses: *He was scared of the words; didn't his actions show how he felt?* His actions were great.

Then came an action that wasn't so great. Brian announced that when I graduated in June we should break up. His reason was that he'd have another year to go at college. During the whole rest of that school year I tried to be the perfect girlfriend, to make myself someone he could never leave.

I developed insomnia and cried all the time. I'm usually a good person but I became this crazy being around Brian. I'd snoop through his stuff to find evidence that he was cheating. I made us take a magazine quiz together on how compatible we were. I said if we got a high score that meant we shouldn't break up. It was a yucky score but I still said we should stay together.

The day before my graduation was Brian's twenty-first birthday. He got horribly drunk and spent our last night together passed out on my bed. I thought, *A year and a half together and this is what I get.* After the ceremony Brian kissed me, said he'd give me a call, and hopped in his car.

I went home to my family for the summer. Brian didn't call so I finally picked up the phone. We only lived an hour apart so we got together one weekend, then the next, and the next. I thought everything was fine but then Brian said we were still broken up.

I took an entry-level advertising job in Michigan to get far away from Brian. I visited him at school one weekend but it was a totally bad scene. I called afterwards and Brian said, "Katy, I want to enjoy my senior year. We're broken up."

After Brian began med school, he'd take internships in random places like Pennsylvania or New Hampshire and call me about once a month. Those were the happiest days for me. I didn't say to myself, "Oh, Brian's in a strange place and lonely, so he's reaching out." I'd fall for it, visit him, and wind up feeling rejected all over again. One time he brought up the possibility of my converting to Judaism, then said that wouldn't be good enough for his father.

The end of this stage happened when I visited him in San Francisco. It had been ten months since our last time together and I couldn't wait to be alone with him. Instead he dragged me out with his friends to a bar. He started talking to a pretty girl and I just lost it. I mean, I blew. I was this bitter, awful, depressed girl who just wanted to make him suffer. I was ugly on the outside because that's how I felt inside.

I got home and started having sex with a series of guys I didn't like. That was how low I'd fallen. I didn't want to open myself up to feeling vulnerable again. Impersonal sex was all I could handle. Then I met a boy who was really cute and who totally wanted to date me. I was so mean to him.

After two miserable years in Michigan I moved back to New York. Brian was there too, and he was dating a girl he liked so much he used the word *girlfriend*. She wasn't Jewish. I said, "How can you do this with another girl after everything we went through?" I was angry but it made me realize Brian wasn't this great guy I'd made him out to be.

It took me four years of being very unhappy but I got over Brian. In the beginning our relationship was happy and healthy. The mistake was saying we were broken up then continuing to sleep together. That really messed me up.

I grew up feeling messed up. My mother had a drinking problem and was always yelling at me. I put up with everything Brian threw at me because it felt familiar and weirdly safe.

My new boyfriend is a great guy. It's the first real relationship I've had since Brian and I split up in college. I hope we stay together but I realize now that life goes on after a breakup. If I survived losing Brian I can survive anything.

Sherry Says

Closure according to *Webster's*: a finish, end; anything that closes.

Without experiencing true closure, that airtight feeling that the fat lady has indeed sung her farewell aria, a couple can become locked into a come-hither/fly-away mode that is an unhealthy mix of passion and pain. For the party that was dumped, the emphasis is on the pain.

Where Brian Erred

Not only couldn't he let Katy down gently, he couldn't bring himself to let her down at all.

Brian went into the relationship emotionally wounded from his blistering bust-up with the Brazilian/Italian maneater. This young man, raised to treat women with respect, wanted to experiment with the notion of having a long-term relationship without actually committing to it. If you hide your heart it can't get broken. But you can still break another person's heart. The couple's first breakup, so traumatic for Katy, barely registered on his radar screen.

Brian was indeed the master of sending mixed messages: One minute he'd be seriously discussing the possibility of Katy's converting to Judaism, the next saying, "We're over when you graduate." Since he knew the depths of Katy's obsession with him, this cavalier treatment of her verged on emotionally criminal behavior. If he were older, more experienced and wise in the fragility of emotional sanity, I'd hold him accountable for not nudging her toward serious psychological counseling. As it was, I deride him for a lack of sensitivity and concern.

Post-breakup, the desire of his "little head" ruled, again and again and again. He knew that each time Katy saw him she prayed it was the beginning of a new beginning. If only Brian had said (and meant) sooner than the San Francisco fiasco, "Katy, it's the end."

Where Brian Shone

To the best of his limited ability, Brian tried to be a good boyfriend. Any red-blooded young male who actually takes a relationship quiz in a woman's magazine deserves some sort of commendation.

Brian attempted time and again to send Katy clear signals that they were not destined to live together happily ever after: *The religious issue matters. You can come visit me but that doesn't mean we're a couple again.* The problem was he instantly subverted those attempts with sexual come-ons. Hopefully, seeing the pain his flip-flop behavior caused Katy has ensured that in the future Brian's words and actions really will match up.

Where Katy Erred

Katy's biggest error was regarding Brian as a savior who could calm the troubled seas of her psyche. Alas, it's easier to look to someone else to *be* our reason for living than to create a life worth living.

A lonely, tumultuous childhood left Katy frantically looking for a lover to make it all better. First she fixated on Tim—not fully letting him go until she hooked up with his successor. Once she was "totally about Brian," she was zero about Katy.

Since she had no core of self, Katy was happy when Brian wanted her; unhappy when he didn't. End of story. This unhealthy dynamic led to extremely self-destructive behavior—from taking drugs, to sleeping with unappealing strangers, to erecting barriers against desirable guys, to picking up and moving to Michigan solely because that's where Brian wasn't. . . . You get the point.

Katy didn't register what Brian was saying ("I will never marry you") because that's not what she wanted to hear. When he crooked a finger in her direction, she didn't think how awful she'd feel after the sure-to-be temporary reunion. Rather, she'd impulsively run into his arms. Each time she saw Brian post-breakup it set her even further back in her recovery. She'd be more depressed and listless about life. And if a person doesn't have at least a tiny spring in her step, it's harder to bounce back from a crushing disappointment.

Where Katy Shone

The gal obviously had a lot of tenacity. She was no quitter. Too bad she wasn't directing her stubborn streak toward learning to both love and to help herself.

Your Love Lesson From This Couple's Breakup

The fever of first love and the sting of first love breakup are sharper than the paroxysms one undergoes after having a few relationship disappointments under one's belt. Survivors of multiple heartbreaks learn that while "love hurts" it's also possible to heal.

The healing, however, can't begin until closure occurs. Closure can't occur until *both* people know it's over. The person who is swinging the ax has to do the deed gently but definitively. Post-breakup, Brian still enjoyed seeing and sleeping with Katy, but his temporary pleasures were pursued at the cost of her ongoing pain.

Mary & Eric

Relationship b: 1990; d: 1993

Chapter 2

Without Forward Motion There's Nowhere to Go But Back

Mary Says

Although Eric was eleven years my junior in some ways he was just like my dad. Both were conservative ex-Navy guys. Thankfully Eric didn't have something else my dad possessed—schizophrenia. I'd lived my youth amid constant turmoil. Subsequently most of my relationships with men had been of a dysfunctional nature.

I was just coming out of that pattern when I met Eric. He's very sweet, great fun, and incredibly dear as a person. I felt instantly comfortable with him. Eric taught me something important. I'd gone through my life feeling responsible just for myself. He showed me that sometimes you have to bear some responsibility for another person.

Shortly before I met Eric my fifteen-year-long untraditional marriage dissolved. My husband, like myself, was a journalist. We lived in different parts of the country. Once a month we'd meet with champagne in our arms, roses in our teeth. The rest of the time we weren't answerable to each other.

In the beginning Eric and I didn't label what we had together. There were no stated boundaries, nor any defined terms. When we'd been dating for around six months I went on assignment to the Mideast and had a fling. I confessed the brief affair to Eric not to hurt him but out of respect. I felt he had a right to know what had happened.

Eric totally flipped out. He shouted, "I have to go find this man!" He started asking me how many men I'd slept with. When I hesitated he said, "Is it more than I can count on one hand?" My saying "yeah" made him flip out again. He jumped to the conclusion I was promiscuous. I rebutted, "You didn't grow up in the sixties like me."

This exhibition of jealousy saddened me. Eric was a lot more judgmental and rigid than I'd imagined. Clearly I'd breached a trust I'd had no awareness of. . . . A trust he regarded as sacred. But I didn't think the breach was insurmountable.

There is so much room for misinterpretation in a relationship. The context of our words and deeds can mean different things to both people. I'd say one thing; Eric might hear another.

To keep things on an even keel I began to quell parts of my personality. I was a lot bolder than Eric was accustomed to. I'm a woman of opinions and substance, probably more than he could handle. I bit my tongue and modified my behavior in ways that make me uncomfortable to remember. I love engaging with strangers; I adore filling my home with good friends. But I indulged a little less in those pastimes when Eric and I were together. And I didn't express my political views quite as fervently. I believe I was the first pro-choice woman Eric ever met.

In some respects we were a breath of fresh air to each other—opening windows into another way of viewing the world. I was this jaded journo who'd seen it all, done it all, and *then* some. Eric's perspective, skewed from teaching elementary-school children, rekindled my innocence. He brought out in me an unexpected lighthearted, playful side. We read children's books together. I still have the music box he gave me that plays "Somewhere Over the Rainbow."

Over the years, though, our relationship became analogous to treading water. I wasn't necessarily eager for children and the suburbs. After a certain point I stopped wondering if he was the person I'd spend my life with. What we shared was wonderful but it became evident we weren't taking the leap off the pier.

In my opinion I shouldered a lot of the burden for keeping the relationship together because I was the one who had damaged it first with my foreign fling, then another affair a year or so later with my first love. I told Eric about this interlude, as was our agreement, and again he took it very hard.

As special a person as Eric was, I realized the basic rigidity of his personality to be something I would ultimately be unable to accept. So the next time I felt an attraction to someone I told Eric we should go our separate ways. This new guy was inconsequential, not someone I felt would become important to me. But meeting him gave me the excuse to move on from a relationship that had run out of steam.

People need to articulate their expectations. A relationship can be a fragile thing. Fault lines can develop that can't be repaired. That's what happened with Eric and me. Eventually both of us moved on.

While I was touched and happy to be invited to his wedding, I admit a part of me will always regret letting a good guy get away.

Eric Says

The three years I spent with Mary taught me, among other things, that I was an extremely jealous person.

Arriving at this realization at age thirty-one was a bit of a shock. I grew up in a strict Baptist home and planned on becoming a minister. I attended seminary but subsequently lost my faith and joined the Navy instead. When my term was over I jumped into marriage with a woman who turned out to be very uptight and controlling. We stayed together nine years and had two children before I found the courage to bail.

Two years after my divorce I met Mary at a neighborhood tavern. She was bohemian, superfriendly and well-traveled—the polar opposite of my ex. I was intrigued.

We slept together on our first date. This was totally out of character for me. But she helped me feel comfortable the morning after.

Mary helped me stretch as a person. I'm a macaroni and cheese kind of guy. She taught me to like fancy stuff. . . . And she taught my eleven-year-old son to cook. She also got me to appreciate singers a lot more eclectic than Perry Como and Barbra Streisand.

A month or so after we began dating, the Desert Storm action commenced and the Naval Reserves called me up to Hawaii for two weeks. I was nowhere near the action but Mary thought that was so cool: her boyfriend going off to war.

I fell in love with her at about the six-month mark. The word marriage was lightly mentioned. That's about the time she went on assignment for two weeks to the Middle East. When Mary returned, we took a walk along the beach and she confessed having had a fling. I got upset. She got upset at my being upset and pointed out that we'd never established our relationship as a monogamous one. I had thought that understanding was implied. This didn't happen in front of her, but I cried.

At that juncture I stopped thinking of the relationship as possibly being forever. Our feelings for each other ran deep but it was clear our outlooks on love were oceans apart. Mary was then forty-three. She'd had an early, brief marriage but I was the first person who'd expected sexual exclusivity from her.

After the dust settled we continued thinking of ourselves as a couple. People sent invitations to "Mary and Eric." By the letter of the law we were monogamous. But we left a trapdoor open by agreeing the relationship was no-strings-attached. We also agreed that if either of us had sex with someone else, we'd let the other know.

During this two-year period I never felt any interest in dating another woman. But there seemed no impetus pushing Mary and me forward.

Our breakup was as amicable as such a thing can be. An old lover came back into Mary's life, someone who made her feel tied up in knots. I didn't approve of the guy. It was obvious he'd hurt her again. Part of me wanted to convince Mary that she and I weren't finished yet. Another part was ready to let her go. That's the part that won. We continued spending time together but no longer ended the evening in bed.

Could Mary and I have wound up married? Although the eagle may be in love with the fish, where would they build the nest? My meaning is that Mary is very different from me. I'm straightlaced. I prefer order and predictability. She's high-energy. At a restaurant she'd constantly chat up people at the next table.

Being with Mary was wonderful in many ways. Staying with her might ultimately have felt too uncomfortable. But she left a lasting legacy in my attitude toward relationships. It's ironic that her sleeping with another man both introduced me to my jealous nature and cured me of that destructive emotion.

I was so glad when Mary came to my wedding last year. After all, she's the person who helped me evolve to the point where I'd recognize the real thing when I found it. And I have found it with my bride.

Sherry Says

In the immortal words of Alvy Singer, aka Woody Allen, in *Annie Hall*: "A relationship is like a shark. It has to constantly be moving forward. What we have here is a dead shark."

Where Mary Erred

Mary uttered these words in hindsight: "People need to articulate their expectations." She should have surmised that her conservative ex-Navy boyfriend might not have as loose an interpretation of sexual boundaries as she, and early on initiated a conversation about this basic relationship issue.

Evidently even a woman as joyously strong as Mary can fall prey to the female tendency of subordinating herself in a relationship. Mary learned later versus sooner that a man incapable of appreciating her fully is ultimately not the man for her. Though it's possible that if she had talked to Eric more freely and regularly about her feelings and what she needed from her partner, he might have been able to work toward a compromise rather than growing increasingly (if silently) intractable.

Mary probably should have ended the relationship once she realized that what she and Eric had on their hands was a dead shark.

Where Mary Shone

Mary jumped off the bad boy bandwagon and at forty-three discovered herself capable of slow dancing with a good guy. This is a *major* accomplishment. And once she and Eric established the if-we-kiss-another-we-tell boundaries of their reconfigured rela-tionship, she did just that.

More kudos to this jaded journo for letting Eric rekindle her inner (playful) child. Even if the shark ultimately ran aground Mary should feel good about having shared fun times with her ex.

Where Eric Erred

Although Mary never pretended to be anything other than a free-spirited child of the sixties, Eric erroneously assumed she shared his views on commitment and fidelity. When that illusion shattered, his feelings of betrayal cut deeper than warranted. He never truly forgave and forgot. If Eric had been able to let this early misunderstanding go, perhaps further gaps that later opened up between he and Mary (i.e.: his discomfort at her joie de vivre) might have been bridgeable rather than more proof that she wasn't *the one*.

Eric's tendency to leap to conclusions was accompanied by a listening problem. How else to explain the assertion that his lover had endured a brief, early marriage? Earth to Eric: When he met then forty-three-year-old Mary, she had recently dis-solved a fifteen-year marriage. He also reported that Mary ulti-mately left him to return to an old love. (I'm assuming Mary's differing accounting of her relationship history is the more accu-rate version.)

In a subconscious way Eric cramped Mary's style. He never said things like, "Stop being so outgoing" but his silent disap-proval caused Mary to occasionally quell the offending aspects of her personality.

He was as ambivalent about taking things to the next level with Mary as he was about cutting the cord. Not knowing what move to make, he made no move and would have continued playing "the relationship drift" game until death them did part.

Where Eric Shone

In addition to being a card-carrying decent man, Eric was capable of (to varying degrees) growth. Under Mary's tutelage he expanded his tastes in music and cuisine and worked hard at curbing his (newly discovered) jealousy. Most important, he grew comfortable with who he was. True, it wasn't admirable that he made Mary feel uncomfortable about fully expressing herself in his presence. But it was great that he discovered his comfort level and drew his line in the sand. He is who he is.

Your Love Lesson From This Couple's Breakup

This three-year relationship was ultimately transitional in nature for both Mary and Eric. Both were fairly recent divorcees and inwardly gun-shy about committing to someone new. Their slow crawl toward possible permanence was stopped in its tracks by a miscommunication and a "betrayal." Afterwards, the couple could never marshal the necessary effort to recover the lost momentum.

Still, both have mostly positive memories of the period they spent together. They laughed and loved together, helped one another grow as individuals, and treated each other with kindness and respect. That is a lovely legacy of a relationship that each will always treasure. However, the relationship might not just be a memory if they hadn't let the window of opportunity close when "Mary and Eric" could have moved forward.

My Biggest Heartbreak and What It Taught Me About Love

Noreen Shea, 44, sells TV programs overseas

It's hard to be politically correct when you break up with a man suffering from terminal cancer. Michael and I met ten years after my divorce. During the eight years we were a couple the only divisive issue we had was that I wanted a child and, with four kids from a previous marriage, he was firm about not wanting to go the father route another time. Then Michael got sick.

After his diagnosis Michael started telling me to leave him. He wanted me to get on with my life. I'm not the type to run out on someone I love. And being with Michael wasn't a hardship. He was still relatively healthy and hopefully would be for many years before the debilitating effects of his form of cancer really took over. We were able to do lots of things together, including travel.

Then Michael became obsessed with making lots of money for his children to inherit. My father had recently died. So I knew what I was talking about when I told him, "What your kids will want after you're gone is not a huge inheritance but memories of times they spent with you."

Michael agreed, but he added, "What will you have when I finally kick, Noreen? Do you want to be fifty years old and walk out of the cemetery, saying, 'Now what am I going to do?'"

He was right. It's been over a year since our breakup. Now that he doesn't have to put up a brave front for me Michael spends intense quality time with his children. Me—I feel like I'm readying myself, that I'm about to meet someone with whom I can build a family.

The cliché that love isn't always enough is all too true. It took more strength to leave Michael than to hang on. But it was the right decision for both of us.

Chapter 3

It's *Not* the Two of You Against the World

Ben Says

My initial attraction to someone is based on her looks. Brittany's red hair and green eyes drew me to her even though when we met, she was sort of dating one of my friends. I was getting out of a five-year relationship myself.

Although we were just twenty years old things got serious right away. I felt very protective of Brittany. She'd had a rough upbringing—her dad is an alcoholic and the rest of her family is verbally abusive. My family is very close-knit.

While I was away at nursing school Brittany had a huge blowup with her folks and needed a place to live. My best friend's parents had a spare room and invited Brittany to stay there. Three weeks into this arrangement there was a fight. They accused Brittany of sneaking into the kitchen and stealing cookies. Because of this stupid argument I lost someone I'd been friendly with since kindergarten. Brittany didn't have many friends of her own so she didn't realize how important mine were to me.

I quit nursing school, came back home, and moved in with Brittany. We declared ourselves officially engaged. That's when the relationship began to derail. I desperately wanted to be a firefighter and that flipped Brittany out. She couldn't deal with the fear that I'd die in a fire. Next, I considered becoming a physical therapist but Brittany vetoed that because I wouldn't make good money. So I enrolled in another nursing school. And oh yes, our sex life, which had been *great*, all but stopped. Brittany kept saying the problem was hers, not mine. But I felt unmanned.

For the first time in my life I was scared of something—marrying Brittany. I went through with it anyway. She didn't sleep with me on our wedding night and there was hardly any intimacy during our honeymoon.

I continued going to nursing school and took a night job as a restaurant manager. I liked the job and was making good money but Brittany hated the late hours so I quit and started working as a security guard.

Brittany had to know where I was every minute. If I wasn't working she wanted me with her. I was exhausted all the time yet she constantly complained I wasn't making enough money or spending enough time with her. On weekends instead of studying or sleeping I'd go with Brittany to flea markets and movies.

Things were very stressful so we went to a marriage counselor. A phrase he said has stuck with me: "If you're not happy with who you are, you can't be happy with someone else."

I was increasingly unhappy with who I was around my wife. She'd strike me and throw her wedding ring in my face. I'm a gentle guy but I got increasingly violent around Brittany. I threw chairs; once I put my fist through the bedroom door. I *never* hit her.

A year into the marriage Brittany started having what seemed like seizures, but all the tests came back negative. The doctors said it was anxiety attacks and upped her dosage of Xanax. A friend of mine said her so-called seizures were ploys to get attention. At this point something clicked. I wanted Brittany to get well so I could leave. I was angry with her and angry with myself for not meeting her expectations. I felt suffocated.

My counselor would say, "Tell her this stuff." I'd be on the floor bawling my eyes out, saying, "Brittany, I don't love you anymore. I don't *like* you." She didn't make any attempt to discuss my emotions or how we could fix things. She'd put her arms around me and say, "There, there. We'll get through it."

Next she developed a thyroid problem. It was treatable but she made out like it was this life-threatening, horrible thing.

I needed badly to get out of the marriage. One night I slept in my car just to avoid going home. Brittany thought I was having an affair with my friend Kim. I was developing feelings for Kim but it didn't turn into a sexual romance until I finally left Brittany.

This sounds cold but I had nothing left to give Brittany. I tried to be the perfect husband. I was so invested in making her happy that I gave up three career paths that might have made me happy. I let her change the way I dress. I put up with no sex. . . . Yet, whenever she beeped me—which was all the time—I'd come running home. She'd say to me, "You're the love of my life. I'd do anything for you," but she didn't do anything to back up her words.

It was easier for me to think about what Brittany wanted than to look deeply inside myself to figure out what I needed. I thought love meant sacrificing yourself for the greater good of the relationship. Kim and I are invested in pleasing ourselves as well as the other person. *If you're not happy with who you are, you can't be happy with someone else.*

Brittany and I never progressed beyond what I consider the first level of love: That "wow" of instant attraction and connection. Once you get to know someone the relationship isn't just about love. It involves communication, trust, honesty, and caring. In the end Brittany and I had only love, and that wasn't enough.

Brittany Says

This sounds goofy but one of the reasons I thought Ben and I were fated to be together was because our initials matched. Almost from the moment we met Ben and I were best friends and completely in love.

It took me a long time to realize how different we were. Education was one of my priorities. I'd watch Ben drop out of school after school after school. Financial stability was also important to me. Ben kept giving me great gifts like a VCR, but when we moved in together I discovered his huge credit card bills. I realized that he wanted to live like the Rockefellers and not work for it.

I grew up in a dysfunctional home and have spent most of my life in counseling. Ben helped me work through a lot of stuff. For example I could never be woken up suddenly without being frightened because my father used to shake me awake and hit me. At the suggestion of my therapist Ben got me up in the middle of the night and gave me ice cream so I'd associate a sudden awakening with something pleasant.

We married in 1996. At our wedding, guests said they'd never seen two people gaze at each other with such incredible devotion. It was a stormy day outside but the sun shone through the chapel window onto my face. Ben and I would have cut our hands and legs off for each other—that's how great our love was.

Before our marriage we made love like bunnies. The longer we were together the worse the sex got. I was afraid of getting pregnant. I'd think, "No, I can't take care of Ben *and* a baby." Because that's how it would have turned out. Ben was so irresponsible.

Our wedding gifts totaled $13,000 and it all went toward bills he'd racked up.

Despite all the home troubles I had a great job as an account specialist for a tech firm and was in line for a fabulous promotion. Then I got sick. *Everything* hurt. My lymph nodes were so swollen the doctors thought it was cancer. One day my limbs started jerking uncontrollably. I wound up in a wheelchair for six months. I couldn't talk. I couldn't walk. Ben was right at my side through all of this.

I gradually got better, even started working again. The first real bump in the road, relationship-wise, came when Ben got close to this girl in his nursing class—Kim. She would page him at 11 P.M. I said that was unacceptable.

Ben started talking about her. "She sticks up for me at school. She really talks to me about things on her mind." I said, "She's six years younger than you are. You're drinking with her and carrying on like you were back in college."

I was disgusted. And he flunked out of yet another nursing school. It was so embarrassing to me that he wasn't going to be anything professionally. I was the husband, wife, and mother rolled into one. I cooked, cleaned, and fulfilled his every whim except in the bedroom. Then I developed thyroid problems. While I was in the hospital I heard him on the phone saying to someone, "I miss you."

Ben took me to a motel at the beach for my birthday but he got drunk and spent the night throwing up in the bathroom. I cried and begged, "I can't change if I don't know what I did wrong."

He said, "All you do is cry. You're pathetic."

Later Ben apologized for ruining my twenty-eighth birthday. But he spent less and less time at home. Finally I said, "This isn't a hotel. You have to leave." We both cried. I packed his bags. He couldn't do it.

One night I drove to the shack he lives in with this girl. It looks like one of those houses where if you huff and puff it'll blow down. I felt very protective of him. I wanted to rush inside, grab him and say, "You can't live like this. Come home." But I left.

The first year without Ben was rough. I'd think, "It's my first snowstorm without Ben. It's my first birthday alone. It's the first anniversary we're not together."

It's been a rough road but Ben and I were never on the same page. He's still trying to figure out his life. He still goes through money like water. He's telling the same story: "I'm gonna get my nursing degree." Everyone in the world has moved on but him.

The one thing I did wrong in my marriage was let my world revolve around my husband. I didn't have friends of my own. Then I wound up feeling overly reliant on Ben.

There are lots of things I regret. I didn't know how to express anger except by hitting Ben verbally and physically. We talked at each other but we never heard what the other person said.

I grew up having money and that didn't buy me happiness. I married for love but that wasn't enough, either. If I remarry it will be to someone who wants a wife, not a mother, someone who wants his partner to be his best friend.

Punch/Counterpunch

BRITTANY: I've learned how to communicate but he hasn't changed.

BEN: My communication with Kim couldn't be better. I've never been happier.

BRITTANY: I wasn't the wife in the marriage. I was the mother.

BEN: Her saying that shows how poor our communication was. She mothered me?! I took care of her.

BEN: Brittany needs a lot of money to be happy. I'm content living with Kim in what Brittany calls a shack.

BRITTANY: He's an irresponsible spendthrift. He has no idea of the value of money.

Sherry Says

Ben and Brittany probably grew up humming songs like "Love Will Keep Us Together." Relying on that tender but precarious emotion to anchor a relationship is romantic but foolhardy. If not supported by things tangible (i.e., basic life comforts) and intangible (i.e., good communication, mutual respect), a relationship can sprout a cancer at its core. This couple grew to be so out of tune with each other that what Ben calls his wife's "anxiety attacks," Brittany labels seizures serious enough to put her in a wheelchair for six months.

Initially this couple loved each other deeply. Thus it is tragic that neither had a clue that both wanted the same thing from marriage: an equal partner and best friend.

Where Ben Erred

He entered into the relationship based on a strong animal attraction. Unfortunately communication between he and Brittany never progressed much beyond the basic gestures and grunts used by four-legged creatures.

The couple's long courtship was punctuated by many arguments, the breakdown of their sexual relationship, and the realization they had different priorities (i.e., he liked to shop 'til he dropped and enjoy life; she needed security on financial and career fronts). Understandably Ben had massive apprehensions about marrying Brittany, but rather than listening to his gut he bit the bullet and prayed that marriage would magically improve his floundering relationship. No one was listening to that prayer.

Although Ben didn't dramatically curb his spending habits he did attempt to change his disposition and goals to suit his wife. Such altruism will inevitably backfire. While it's admirable to compromise on certain goals and issues, a person who devalues his intrinsic nature for his partner will soon resent his partner.

This resentment turned Ben into someone who abused his wife on her birthday, regularly stayed out all night, and had an intimate relationship with another woman. Even Ben would admit he was at least *emotionally* unfaithful during the marriage to his legal and spiritual partner.

Where Ben Shone

Ben is clearly capable of deep devotion. He was willing to try marital therapy, help Brittany overcome personal demons (such as her fear of being awoken in the middle of the night), and to be at her side during medical emergencies.

He also grew wise enough to realize that a relationship isn't just about love.

Where Brittany Erred

She was childishly idealistic about relationships: Matching initials does not a happy marriage make.

Her dysfunctional upbringing left her with something akin to posttraumatic stress syndrome. She expected the worst. If a bill wasn't paid right away, calamity would follow. If her husband became a firefighter, he'd die in a blaze. It is no surprise that she suffered stress-related illnesses.

To offset her fears, she tried to control as much of her world as possible. Ergo her doomed efforts to turn Ben into the husband she thought he should be.

Communication was this couple's Waterloo. Instead of telling Ben she feared sex with him would result in pregnancy, Brittany allowed him to believe she found him undesirable. She was no better at listening to Ben's point of view. Just telling someone, "There, there," when he's pouring out his demons doesn't make him feel *heard*, nor does it address the problem. Neither does punching, cursing, or throwing your wedding ring.

Where Brittany Shone

She's overcome a lot in her life (e.g., dysfunctional childhood, medical calamities) and is clearly working to become a better person. She tried to nurture Ben to the best of her ability.

Your Love Lesson From This Couple's Breakup

Ben said it: *If you're not happy with who you are, you can't be happy with someone else.* You can't look to your partner to define you, complete you, or give your life zip and meaning. You can't take away the pain and fear your partner has suffered in life, nor expect him or her to "make up" for all the pain and fear you have suffered.

You should nurture each other, be each other's best friend, helpmate, and cheerleader. You should also (tactfully and lovingly) call each other on your "stuff." But don't, as Brittany did, push your partner into a box labeled "perfect mate." There is no such animal. Your lover isn't here to do your bidding. Nor are you here to do his.

Rather than being joined at the hip, allow each other breathing space to grow. The more dynamic your life apart is (in terms of jobs, hobbies, friends) the more you'll have to share with each other when you're cuddling in bed at night.

Bottom line: To succeed as a couple, you can't just be a couple, but two individuals who each bring love, empathy, trust and the ability to communicate and compromise to the relationship.

Chapter 4

One Loves, The Other Is Loved—Not

Barbara Says

I met Samuel at a gay bar in New York. A gay guy friend and I went in for a drink and spied Samuel pouring drinks. I bet my friend that Samuel was straight. The bet paid off for me—big-time.

Samuel was newly arrived from Australia and the only work he could get was as a bartender. He seemed very theatrical—his hair flowed to his butt and he wore a skimpy T-shirt. His accent was cute and I *loved* the fact that he taught ballroom dancing.

I was twenty-seven and not looking for any heavy relationship stuff. But Samuel and I hit it off. Shortly after we met he went back to Australia for six weeks. We wrote back and forth and had ridiculously long and expensive phone calls.

When Samuel came back he spent all his time at my apartment. He'd bring me flowers, write me poetry . . . I didn't realize he had officially moved in until a friend called and said, "Whose voice is that on your answering machine? His accent is so sexy."

I'd always been a strong, stable, independent individual who handled stress well. But Samuel caught me at a low point. My parents, who I always felt had a happy marriage, divorced suddenly. I was *totally* distraught. Plus, I was still smarting over a boyfriend who'd broken my heart. So it felt nice to have this fascinating man from Down Under charge in and take over my life. And he found comfort at having someone close at hand in a strange country.

Although our sexual chemistry wasn't great we had a solid emotional and intellectual connection. And we were of like minds when it came to big life issues like abortion and capital punishment.

There wasn't a moment when I said to myself: "Oh, he's the one for me." Our marriage nine months after we met was due to circumstantial reasons. Samuel had a limited visa. With the proper work papers a lot more doors would open for him. The ceremony was at City Hall. It didn't occur to either of us to go on a honeymoon. Nothing changed except that we had a license.

A year after the marriage we started an import/export business. The business became our baby. We poured everything into it. It was clear that no matter what the personal dynamic was between us our mutual commitment to the business was 100 percent.

And I did love being with Samuel. He's one of the most memorable characters I know. For instance, if we were riding in the subway late at night and there'd be frightening-looking individuals at the other end of the train smoking, he'd have no qualms about walking up to them and saying, "Hey mates, that bothers my nose. Would you mind?"

Sometimes when you admire a person's intrinsic qualities you mistake your feelings for something else. I found Samuel intriguing on many levels and I thought that was enough to make me happy. But socializing with other couples who were clearly in love caused waves of loneliness to wash over me. No matter how great Samuel and I were together—the passionate heart of a male/female relationship didn't exist between us.

During our last year and a half together sex dwindled to the point where we were like the *Odd Couple*'s Oscar and Felix—roommates only. But neither of us looked elsewhere. Cheating wasn't in our makeup.

I started to feel angry with myself for making such a big mistake. I was angry with Samuel too. It was suffocating being with him 24/7. We began having lots of *very* toxic arguments. None of them even began to clear the air between us.

My turning point came the weekend I spent visiting my college roommate. We charted the positives and negatives of my marriage. There were many positives. But you can't manufacture chemistry.

Samuel and I didn't have a specific "breakup" conversation. But there was an unspoken mutual awareness that came to fruition right around the time Samuel's parents paid us a three-week visit from Australia. After they left I packed up and moved to my sister's place. I came back to the house the next day because that was also my workplace. Over two years after the divorce, we still work together running our business.

It took me nearly two years before I felt ready for a relationship. I needed time to figure out what I'd been doing the last six years. I realize now that I shouldn't have clung to Samuel like a life raft after my parents' divorce. I should have gotten my act together before jumping into a relationship.

Samuel did teach me to be a better communicator. When I'm hurt my tendency is to shut down and crawl into a hole. Or I blow up and say hurtful things. Probably our best times together were when we were dancing cheek-to-cheek. Those tangos and waltzes felt sexier than sex.

I stayed in the marriage so long because I kept wishing it would get better. I should have accepted that the love I feel for Samuel is brotherly.

I'm in a relationship now that has all the passion my marriage lacked. We're lighthearted together, constantly laughing—and looking at him makes me want to buy half the lingerie featured in the Victoria's Secret catalog.

The truth is that Samuel and I are brilliant together as business partners but abysmal as husband and wife. If I hadn't ended it, we'd be like two old farts roaming around an overgrown garden.

Samuel Says

I have a tendency to fall in love quickly but all my relationships before Barbara were crash and burn: over in three months.

When Barbara looked at me in the bar, her smile struck my heart with the force of a bullet. I knew this woman could get anything she wanted from me. She was exactly my age, beautiful, a ferociously talented sculptor possessed of a combination of stability and fragility that was irresistible. We went home together that night, and, except for business trips, I didn't leave her side for six years.

I'm very intense, very passionate, and knew instantly that Barbara was what I call my "immortal beloved"—the one who will always haunt my heart. Barbara loved me back but she is much more inhibited and reserved than I. It was a lot of work trying to open her up. Passion involves knowing what you want sexually and going after it. Barbara didn't feel deserving of good sex so she never asked for what she needed.

I told her bluntly, "You've got to make yourself number one. Be selfish about getting the love you need."

She didn't take to this kind of talk too well. Flattery of any kind made her uncomfortable. If I called Barbara beautiful—and she has looks most women would kill for!—she would be upset the rest of the day.

There were huge cultural differences between us. Australians enjoy freedom. Before coming to the United States, I'd been on a year-long, round-the-world "walkabout." New Yorkers are very regimented. The way Barbara takes a trip is by planning it beforehand for six months—budgeting for it, organizing . . .

I never tried to change any aspect of Barbara's personality. But she looked at me with the fervor of Henry Higgins discovering Eliza Doolittle. Nothing satisfied her from my style of dressing to my feeling no need to amass a lot of money. She made it clear I'd better develop a career more solid than ballroom dancing and bartending.

Gradually I realized that even if I made the changes Barbara wanted, she wouldn't be happy. Things got radically worse three years into the relationship when we moved in with her mother to save money for a down payment on a house.

I became part of the background to my wife. I found myself living in a battlefield peopled with screaming women. Barbara's sister and grandmother were also on the premises, constantly bitching about anything and everything. If a tradesman didn't come to make a repair on time, Barbara's mother would raise the roof with her decibel level. I'd finally make the repair just to restore a temporary peace.

Barbara and I didn't have sex once during the year we lived there. I'm not an animal, but I love sex. My wife and I didn't even kiss anymore, just a peck on the cheek like sister and brother. This was killing me. During this period I wrote a book of poems to Barbara—poems tinged with frustration and sadness.

I made no demands on her and she made no effort to please me. I retreated into a shell, sat on my feelings, and experienced zero needs. Oh, maybe once or twice I lost my temper in a small way. But I knew if I said things that upset Barbara, there'd be hell to pay. My wife held grudges like a camel holds water.

This was the worst period of my life. Barbara and I talked

about separating three or four times while under her mother's roof. But I fought for the marriage. I grew up playing competitive sports and it's not over even with one minute left on the clock.

Finally we got our own place—an old colonial farmhouse. Things between us didn't improve. I lost my stamina. I realized I had to go out and get a life. I don't want to wake up at eighty and say, "Gee, I've been miserable for sixty years."

Yet, I'm such an idealist it would have made me happy to be given the opportunity to die miserably at Barbara's feet. In the greatest love stories, people walk through fire to achieve romantic perfection.

I got no satisfaction from the marriage because I could never make Barbara happy. I'd cook, clean, do the laundry, work extra jobs to make money to buy her gifts. She never saw what I did, only what I didn't do.

In a relationship two people look out the same window but see different views. I still love Barbara to my core and wonder how I could have made things turn out differently. Maybe if we hadn't moved in with her mom, or if I hadn't invited her to join the business, or if I'd tried even harder to fill her needs we'd still be together.

Due to our company we still see each other all the time. It's like being married without the sex. Come to think of it, it's just like our marriage.

Sherry Says

The major dysfunction here (and it's a biggie) is that Barbara thought she was in a business arrangement while Samuel believed himself to be in a romantic novel—the one where the guy, abandoned by his lover, hurls himself under a train.

In Samuel's case the figurative leap to doom occurred time

after time during the relationship. The more he prostrated himself before his wife, the less she noticed the "sacrifices" he made in the name of love.

Barbara made sacrifices too, as her commitment and love grew tenfold during the marriage. Only all the "folds" were directed toward her import/export business and none toward her husband.

Where Barbara Erred

Barbara made one of the oldest mistakes in the book by choosing a marriage partner when she was a weak, vulnerable facsimile of her true self. "I was at a low point." Initially, she looked at Samuel as her protector, someone who would swoop in and *take charge*. Once she felt strong enough to take back her life she was anchored to a husband she admired but didn't love or sexually covet.

He was also a husband she didn't really bother getting to know. So unaware was Barbara that she was Samuel's "beloved immortal" that she assumed he married her out of a need to have a best buddy in a strange country and get a visa. Post-ceremony she barely noticed his feverish attempts to please her. Barbara was so busy concentrating on the things she didn't have that she completely missed what she had.

It's not a moral crime not to have the hots for your partner. It is heinous, however, to treat your lover like a brother. Better to get out, leaving the other person some dignity rather than institute the ultimate carnality-crusher: moving your husband into your mother's home. And it is sadly fascinating that while Samuel devoted chapter and verse to the effects of this address change on the marriage, it didn't register on Barbara's relationship Richter scale of destruction.

A major error of Barbara's was hoping that the passage of time would magically heal the relationship's woes. When it didn't (surprise!), instead of communicating her feelings and fears to her husband, she repressed them. The result: insidious anger that ate away at anything that was still good and holy at the heart of the marriage.

Where Barbara Shone

She is obviously capable of working with a mate—even if it's primarily on business affairs. Despite the mounting personal problems between her and Samuel, they launched a successful business. It is to her credit that postdivorce she and her ex maintain a workable friendship.

I also applaud Barbara's decision to not leap into a postdivorce tryst, rather to take her time to analyze her part in the breakdown of a union that was supposed to last *so long as you both shall live*.

Where Samuel Erred

His outsize passion led him to make foolhardy moves. When not bounding up to frightening-looking individuals on a deserted train demanding they put out cigarettes, he was degrading himself for the love of a woman who barely knew he was alive.

To him love involved a torrid trinity: sacrifice, selflessness, sorrow. If it don't hurt, it can't be the real thing.

While his wife made no effort to please him, Samuel took pride in having made no demands on her. His romantic idealism was his Achilles' heel. It blinded him from realizing that a woman who thinks she's doing him a favor when she proffers her cheek for a buss is a bust as a wife. His blindness to the potential joys of a partnership between equals cheated Barbara as well. She was forced to watch the man she'd married for his strength transfigure into a mouse. No wonder he became background to her; that's all he was to himself.

Samuel mistook the exquisite agony of existing in a state of perpetual longing and loss for the unavoidable side effects of experiencing a great love.

Where Samuel Shone

He is capable of great emotion, great loyalty, and great spurts of giving. This is a man who knows how to please (or to die trying).

Your Love Lesson From This Couple's Breakup

There was a crucial misbalance in the depth of emotion and effort between this couple. The dichotomy created when one person loves while the other is loved is the stuff of poetry, song, literature, and film. However, it is *not* the stuff of viable relationships.

My Biggest Heartbreak and What It Taught Me About Love

Goddess Lydia, 40, Internet radio DJ

The father of my child succeeded at splintering my heart. We were together six years. I wanted to get married. He didn't . . . until he met another woman.

When he split I was devastated. Even though both of us were miserable in the relationship I would never have left. I'm a very loyal person.

It took me a few years to work through the anger and grief and to realize that the breakup was actually a gift. My ex was incapable of emotion, so I had taken on his feelings in addition to mine. The more I felt, the more he retreated emotionally. Consequently we loved each other to the worst of our abilities. The damage this caused wasn't just to me, but to him. Neither of us could make the other happy. The only way he could bring himself to leave this arid standoff was to be unfaithful.

Eventually I was able to step back and look at the limitations of this person I loved so deeply and for so long. He used to say, "Why do you love me? I'm so shallow and you're so deep." I should have paid attention to his assessment and run for cover. He truly doesn't know how to be a man on an emotional level and it's not my job to teach him. I've stopped blaming him for not being the man I wanted him to be. I'm not the woman he wanted me to be either.

For years whenever I dropped my son at the house my ex shares with his wife, a part of me died. She's a nice woman. But she has a lot of money and gives my child all the things I can't afford. It took everything I had in me not to badmouth her to my son, but to instead pick up the phone and rant to my therapist or a friend about all this injustice. Now I realize the breakup has given my son a gift as well: he has another house where he feels safe and he has more people to love him.

The truth: My ex did me a favor by walking. It's my fervent belief that if I had stayed in that unhealthy relationship the stress of living in such misery would have eventually killed me.

Ed & Jan

Relationship b: January 2000; d: July 2000

Chapter 5

If Both Partners Need to Be on Top, the Relationship Goes Belly-Up

Ed Says

Jan picked me up. She stomped up to me at a bar, stuck out her hand, and said something witty. I was quite impressed. I'm this black, blue-collar guy who works for a utility company. Jan's white *and* white collar. We exchanged business cards and later hooked up for lunch.

Before Jan, I had three serious relationships including an eight-year marriage that ended four years ago. I've got two kids. Jan's forty-five—three years older than me—but I grooved off the confident way she handled herself.

Jan *claims* to be low maintenance but she's always freaking about her career. I seem to attract professional women who want someone to anticipate their needs and have the correct response prepared: "Oh, baby. You're great. You're gonna be okay." I don't have enough game to lie. I don't want to hear about my girlfriend's job.

I was seeing another woman when I first started hanging with Jan. Two weeks in, I decided Jan had the better package. I was cool being exclusive with Jan. But I felt she was doing her thing with other guys, which was fine.

We went on outings, to dinner parties, the ballet. . . . Jan paid for a lot of the ritzy stuff. That's just the way it rolled up. I'm not a gigolo but a guy like me can't do $120 dinners more than once a month. Jan doesn't like cheap things.

She was so nice to be around and made me feel good about myself. Jan's a very informed person and every word out of her mouth is something I didn't know. She'll read a four-hundred-page book in an hour and a half. I was her studly little brother dude, which was okay. I don't claim to be anything other than what I am. Give me football, good sex, and a sandwich. Jan needs a little more stimulation.

She's a white girl, me a black guy. Yet I'm the right-wing Republican who believes in God but not in abortion or homosexual love. She has the opposite beliefs. She's opposite in *lots* of ways. We dated six months and she doesn't even remember my phone number. It took me a day to memorize hers.

I don't drink. Jan's a bottle-a-night girl. When Jan's a little soused I'm as smart as she is. And she gets adorably girlish. I have mental pictures of us that I'll keep forever: her smile the time we took salsa lessons; The night we stayed up until 2 A.M. talking about an idea for an Internet company. In my heart I didn't think it would work out between us but there were times when things really clicked.

We had lover problems. I'm a big hitter but I guess I wasn't swinging the bat right for her. I'd strike out a lot. And she'd refuse to wear this hot, red skirt I bought for her. Jan weighs 150 pounds and thinks she's heavy. I'd say, "Girlfriend, you are not fat."

Even though I live in California, I'm a thug from the Newark projects. I speak loud and obnoxious. When I'd curse, Jan would call it emotional abuse. I was just doing my thing. God understood.

For six months I wanted her to commit and she left it hanging. She needed to be cautious. She made statements like a politician: Nothing important was really declared. She'd swear I was special to her but I didn't feel it. Our fights got really bad. I try to forget the bad stuff, but one time I think I left her stranded downtown without a car.

What broke us up was a Fourth of July weekend. I said, "Let's set something up for the weekend." She agreed, then kept putting me off, saying she might have to work during the holiday. So for the first time in nearly six months I went out with another lady. I wished it was Jan I was hanging out with but I wasn't going to blow the whole holiday.

After the weekend she said, "I'm gone." I let her go. As soon as Jan said she didn't believe in God, I should have been outta there. The most important thing to have in common is faith. Without that, you don't have a purpose in life.

I'm sorry now I didn't listen harder when she had work problems. I'm also sorry I didn't lower the volume of my voice. I'm way wilder than she is. I need someone who can keep me at home. For a long time I hoped that someone would be Jan.

I've dated so many girls in my life it's embarrassing. I gotta find me a good one who shares the same core beliefs. Then we can sit back and watch the flowers bloom.

Jan Says

The night I met Ed, I was one of three white women hanging out at a black bar. I was drawn to him by the interesting contrasts in his character. Here was this gorgeous hunk of man sporting a bald head and the most dreadful outfit—a feminine, white see-through shirt, black leather jeans, and scads of loud jewelry. I made a comment to him and we wound up talking about coral and molluscan!

We exchanged business cards and the next day Ed E-mailed me the URL for his Web site. It featured hard-core pictures of his penis. It was beyond flirt. But I still met him for lunch.

I guess I'm a serial monogamist—I lived with one man for five years; another for three. All the guys I'd been involved with were educated, intellectual, and career-oriented.

Ed broke that mold! He personifies the path I didn't take in life. While I spend hardly any time on my hair, makeup or clothes Ed puts an enormous effort into effecting his package. He projects the aura: *I am a mindless cupcake.* Once I mentioned something about his nipples being hot and he got them pierced in an effort to be pretty for me.

Ed and I have both faced discrimination in our lives so we're insecure and hugely invested in guarding our power base. From the beginning I adored Ed but never admitted it. Yes, even though he said "I love you" on the fourth date and hinted that he wanted to marry me. My response was that said it was way too early to be monogamous. I needed to keep a rein on my emotions. He countered that I saw him as just a big, black stud. I said, "You can't send someone a picture of your c— and not be thought of as a sex symbol."

Ed is funny and gregarious. For the first two months we were very happy. I had more money but he'd feed me well and constantly bring me things: flowers, a pair of shoes.

There was an even balance of power between us. Ed was dominant sexually and I was on top in terms of intelligence and education. He and I were each other's missing other half.

I was careful not to knock him down. I didn't make fun of his New Jersey accent or ask him to take out the nipple rings when we went swimming. However, although he claimed to appreciate the conservative intellectual that I am, he tried to turn me into a hoochie mama—asking me to call him "Daddy," wear tight red dresses and shiny shirts.

Things began to degenerate when he pressured me to have unsafe sex. I was upset that he'd rather put my life at risk than sacrifice a 3 percent improvement on the intensity of his orgasm. I became frigid and our sex life dwindled to nothing. He finally agreed to take an HIV test. We were both negative and went back to having safe sex. But I couldn't relax into lovemaking anymore.

Rather than trying to intellectually problem solve our sexual impasse and ask, "Baby, what can I do to make you happy?" Ed got defensive. I tried to explore with him the possibility that our issue was about control, not sex. In my opinion he withheld carnal pleasure from me because he knew sexual prowess was his most powerful attribute.

His mean streak came out with a vengeance. We'd have a fight on the phone, he'd yell, "We're done," and slam down the receiver. I hated when he raised his voice or used vulgarity. I'd be so miserable, then I'd look out my kitchen window and there he'd be in some adorably incongruous getup scat-singing a bebop song.

The horrible thing was that I saw the patterns, realized the ways we were sabotaging the relationship, yet I was unable to talk to him about it.

I had frequent-flier miles saved up and wanted to use them to treat Ed to a fishing trip over the Fourth of July weekend. While we were discussing arrangements he got verbally abusive yet again on the phone, screaming, "Goddamit, I can't leave Thursday night. I have to work Friday morning." Then he hung up on me. I called the travel agent to cancel the plans. This was a punishment for me, too. I'd been looking forward to our getaway but I couldn't reward someone for bad behavior.

I saw two old boyfriends over that weekend and I know Ed

was with a woman. That didn't bother me. I'm looking for something deeper than sexual monogamy. I'm interested in the quality of our feelings and intentions toward each other. We had an incandescent union but I got tired. I don't want that much drama. The conversation where I broke up with Ed also marked the first time I said I loved him.

Deep down Ed and I *get* each other. Our underlying neurosis meshed. When he held me, I felt gorgeous. I felt loved. But verbally we couldn't communicate.

Perhaps if I'd given him reason to trust me early on he would have been less inclined to lash out whenever he felt insecure. He had the balls to put his feelings out there. I didn't. If I had it to do over, I'd have made a commitment to him. We both loved *and* liked one another but lacked the ability to put it together.

If Ed and I had learned to communicate properly we could have spent our energy fighting the world instead of each other.

Punch/Counterpunch

ED: Why couldn't she wear the red dress that made her look so hot?

JAN: My wearing the stupid dress would have proven he was important enough to me that I'd wear a garment I hated.

ED: After six months together, she hadn't memorized my telephone number.

JAN: Give me a break. His number was programmed into my cell phone's speed dial.

JAN: His belief in God is a smoke screen. He doesn't go to church. He doesn't treat the people in his life—his children included—with kindness.

ED: Faith is the most important thing in the world to me.

ED: All I want is to find a good woman.

JAN: When he finds a good woman, he'll try to turn her into a ho.

JAN: He valued me so little that he tried to force me to have unsafe sex.

ED: Whoa, lawdy!!!!!!!!! Talk about selective memories! I wish I knew how to shrug off all responsibility for my actions. I'm done with this. I'm too Neanderthal to continue this topic. . . .

Sherry Says

Outwardly Ed and Jan seem like an odd couple—the black, blue-collar guy and the white, white-collar gal. They were intoxicated rather than irritated by each other's differences. And on a subterranean level these two connected utterly. Yet their relationship went belly-up in six months.

The overriding reason for the duo's demise: If you insulate your heart more ferociously from your lover than a football team guards the ball from the opposing team, no matter how many times you score, there is no winner.

Where Ed Erred

Memo to Ed: Nowhere in the *How to Romance an Intellectual, Accomplished Woman* manual does it suggest treating her to pictures of your private parts before you've broken bread together. Although an X-rated version of said manual might okay such a salacious act it is still best not to be so cocksure that a sighting of yourself in the cyber-buff will win the lady.

Opening gambits aside, once Ed's relationship with Jan was under way, he repeatedly derailed it by displaying a defensive attitude of impenetrable proportions. Jan would state what she needed from him (i.e., a listening ear about her work woes, not to use vulgarity or a raised voice) and instead of trying to deliver the goods, he'd feel attacked, rant, and pull away.

While God understands Ed's need *to do his own thing*, Ed's ex isn't as evolved as the Lord. Jan needed her lover to step outside his worldview and see hers.

Where Ed Shone

This "mindless cupcake's" anthem could be, "I've Gotta Be Me." He is comfortable with, as his former lover put it, "effecting his package." Bully for him that he was proud, rather than intimidated, by Jan's professional success, superior intellect, etc. He also reveled (at least initially) in helping his partner cue in to her feminine power. He knew how to make this high-powered woman feel beautiful, sexy, and adored.

Most importantly he's in touch with his feelings, unafraid to put his heart on the line. Ed saw whom he wanted and let her know it. Unfortunately, as the previous section illustrates, his courtship methodology left something to be desired.

Where Jan Erred

While it's dumb to be a fool for love, it's equally unwise to always keep your brain on full alert. Jan's tendency to intellectualize every aspect of the love affair helped divorce her from emotion. Conclusive proof: Jan's being unable to gift Ed with the ultimate verbal kiss ("I love you") until the day she gave him the kiss-off.

She accused Ed of responding defensively whenever she tried to get him to change a behavior pattern. Yet her pattern was to force her lover (a "simple" guy whose idea of bliss was "football, good sex, and a sandwich") to attack their problems from an intellectual perch. If Jan truly wanted to stop sabotaging the relationship she could have suggested a few sessions of couple's therapy to help them work on their communication impasse.

Although she accepted Ed's nipple rings, flashy wardrobe, and lack of material success as part of *his package*, she took his loud tones and occasional vulgar language as a personal affront; proof that he didn't value her package. During the fatal Fourth of July argument, if she could have told him how hurt she was by his angry manner instead of canceling the trip and being evasive about seeing him over the weekend, their story might have had a happier ending.

Where Jan Shone

An iconoclastic thinker, Jan doesn't limit herself to the kind of man a mother, friend, or employer thinks would look best on her arm. This self-described "serial monogamist" has been there, done that. Subsequently she is willing to go outside the box to find the man who succors her inner and outer layers.

She is also capable of handling with equanimity her lover's idiosyncrasies (i.e., E-mailing photos of intimate parts of his package, nipple rings) and discerning enough to know that without emotional fidelity, sexual faithfulness isn't enough to hold a relationship together. However, that doesn't mean that monogamy isn't a desirable state of affairs for a couple to attain.

Your Love Lesson From This Couple's Breakup

Don't let a power trip trip up your chance to succeed at love.

Ed and Jan's romance was done in by their egos. I define ego as that little being inside us that needs to be loved to exact specifications: *If he really loved me he'd never hang up on me. If she really loved me, she'd wear that red dress even though it makes her feel fat.*

Ego sings a mind-numbing aria: *me, me, me.* The refrain is:

Enough about you. What about me? A couple who can't get beyond their individual egos can only see their reflected selves in each other's eyes. They're so scared of being blindsided by the other person that they're blind as to who the other person really is. The relationship becomes about control. As Jan said, "Instead of battling the world, we battled each other."

Alix & Ed

Relationship b: 1965 d: 1992

Relationship b: 1993 to present

Chapter 6

Cancel the Out Clause

Alix Says

Many divorced people would go back to their original spouses if they weren't so full of pride. It's not like they wanted to separate in the first place. Most divorces happen out of a sense of despair and hopelessness. For my husband and me, splitting up was a last resort. There seemed nothing left to do.

Ed and I met on a blind date in April 1965, three days after I turned eighteen. He was my second or third boyfriend—I can't remember exactly which. I do remember that Ed was cute, kind, a great friend always willing to do me a favor. We both came from poor families in Detroit, which helped us really connect on an emotional level. Six months after we met, Ed proposed in my parents' study.

I hoped my marriage would be as rock-solid as the one between Mom and Dad. They were together forty-five years.

Mom ruled the roost. Dad was more or less dependent on her wisdom and judgment.

The wedding in December 1968 was small but wonderful. Immediately afterward, Ed started medical school. I taught elementary school and attended grad school two nights a week. Every Saturday we'd clean the apartment and grocery shop. Thinking back, it was very sweet. Our life was a joint effort.

Our first baby was born in 1972. That's when things started to change. I was concentrated on home and child while Ed's focus became work. Our lives diverged onto parallel tracks. We didn't understand the importance of spending time together. What we did understand was the importance of being consumers. We were impressed not just by the stuff, but by our ability to buy such a bounty. Though it was a constant thorn in my side that Ed never seemed to "get" the kinds of gifts I wanted him to buy me.

During the '70s and '80s Ed and I continued becoming more and more alienated from each other. I didn't know exactly what was missing, just that I ached for something more. I looked to friends to fill the emotional void. Sex became more perfunctory, less intense unless we were angry with each other. Then we'd summon up some passion.

In 1985 at my suggestion, Ed and I tried marital therapy. We went once a week for a year and a half, but our marriage wasn't improved one iota. I'm a couples counselor now. Looking back, our therapist went wrong by not being confrontational. She was helpful to Ed and me singly: I received permission to go back to school and get on with my life. But as a unit Ed and I weren't challenged. The therapy never forced us to get to the heart of what was going on in our marriage.

The relationship floated along. We'd have periods of fights, then silences . . . sometimes the latter lasted weeks at a time. There were certain topics that never came up: Ed's feelings, his family, how he did or didn't deal with relationships in his life.

When I filed for divorce in January 1992, I can't tell you how many people asked, "Why don't you just go out and have an affair?" That never crossed my mind, or Ed's. But it's no accident that I took steps to end the marriage in the same six-month period my eldest daughter went off to college and I had to put my father in a nursing home. It was increasingly evident how important time was and how quickly it was running out. I felt a real urgency to do something about my situation.

Ed was in stunned disbelief. Even though I'd threatened divorce in the past, he never thought I'd do it. Our lifestyle was so affluent—a beautiful house, beautiful cars, clothes and jewelry, expensive vacations. Ed didn't think I'd walk away from all that.

The divorce attorneys saw the opportunity to make a lot of money and turned what should have been a fairly easy situation into something ugly. My lawyer's bullying fear tactics made me afraid I'd wind up with nothing. He insinuated Ed was hiding assets so he could cheat me out of what was legally mine.

While this was going on I started a whirlwind romance with a man I'd known for years. Ed was dating, too, which didn't bother me. I felt the new woman in his life would soon discover how aggravating he was!

As the weeks went on and I continued seeing this other man, it began gnawing at me that there were so many things about my personality he wasn't picking up on. This ranged from the type of flowers I enjoyed receiving to intimacies I preferred in bed. I had to articulate my needs to him, and I realized I hadn't articulated to Ed. I'd assumed he'd just know what things would make me happy. In addition, my new beau had qualities I didn't like, such as being frugal, that made me appreciate Ed.

Three months after the separation Ed called and asked if he could come home. I said yes, and told the attorney to stop the divorce action. It didn't take long until the same power struggles and patterns emerged. We fought about money, in-laws . . . plus, Ed was still so angry with me for leaving him that any little thing would cause a huge feud.

Six months after moving back in, Ed walked out. This time he filed for divorce.

It's an understatement to say that 1992 was a tough year. My dad died and the divorce was finalized. Yet along with the devastation was a sense of freedom. For the first time there was no man underfoot second-guessing me or telling me what to do. I opened a private counseling practice and began dating again. I bought a new house as well as a new car. There seemed no need to ever remarry. I had control over my life.

In April 1993 Ed and I had to go to court. There was a check for mutual fund dividends that required both our signatures. Ed told the judge, "I'll sign this if Alix will have coffee with me." I said okay.

We went downstairs to the courthouse cafeteria and sat across from each other. Ed started to cry. This was the first time I'd seen him shed tears since his father died. He talked about how mad he was, and also how miserable.

That was the beginning. We started dating. At the time I was seeing several people, including a much younger man. This was different. Ed was different. So was I. I'd learned to be responsible for myself, to ask for what I needed. I was also able to see Ed more clearly. He wasn't just someone who continually disappointed me. He was a solid, kind, compassionate guy. I saw all over again why I'd married him.

We expect our partners to do the things for us that we should be doing for ourselves. The first time around I assumed Ed would take care of me financially, emotionally, and physically. For example if I was going shopping late at night it was his job to accompany me for protection. Since I'd been invested in people liking me, it had always been up to Ed to fight my battles—with his family, my family, neighbors. I hadn't realized it was my job to take care of Ed as well.

It helped that I was now earning my own money. I respected myself for it, and so did Ed. He'd been sure when we split that I'd fall apart. I had thrived.

When we began dating I suggested we take a workshop led by Harville Hendrix, Ph.D., who wrote *Getting the Love You Want: A Guide for Couples*. The communication skills Ed and I learned that weekend were phenomenal. We discovered that what had been missing between us was empathy. Learning to put ourselves in each other's shoes forced Ed and I out of our narcissism.

Twenty years after we met Ed and I found ourselves in the beginning of the love phase where you finish each other's sentences and have great sex 24/7. In December 1993 we remarried. Our children of course were delighted.

An essential piece that's different this time around is the unspoken agreement that we will never divorce. Splitting up is not an option! Having that level of commitment forces us to deal with each other come hell or high water. There is a feeling of safety. You are never going to be left.

We're not floating anymore. We're not alienated or lonely. We spend time with each other, we're direct about how we feel, and we validate the other's opinion. For instance, in the old days I would have objected to Ed's habit of seeing his mother only three times a year. I'd have tried to get him to spend more time with her. Now I say that I understand why this is comfortable for him and back off.

Am I sorry we divorced? Yes and no. We missed a lot of time together but being apart helped us come to value each other in ways that used to seem impossible.

Ed Says

I felt very alone growing up. My father was always screaming. Mom's fear of him made her very passive. My only sibling was learning disabled. I started working part-time jobs when I was ten and tried to be home as little as possible.

I started dating at a young age. My first real girlfriend moved away when we were in the eighth grade. I immediately hooked up with someone else who moved away when we entered junior high school.

During my first eight weeks of college, friends set me up on eight blind dates. Alix was number eight. There was no number nine. I'm not a spiritual person but I felt that my beloved grandfather had sent Alix to me from heaven.

She was in her last year of high school but I felt connected with her right away. We went bowling. I said, "I'll spot you fifty pins." She bowled 201—my kind of woman. She, however, was so impressed with me that she called me by the wrong name!

Still, we quickly became a couple. After our marriage we were both very busy: me in med school, Alix as the world's most devoted teacher. By the time I'd finished school and my residency, we'd been married eight years and had two kids.

I was so consumed with work that the thought of working on the relationship didn't enter my mind. I didn't know what an "emotional feeling" was . . . or much care.

Alix was in a different place. Subsequently we'd argue a lot— even about the way we argued. We wouldn't talk for days or weeks, then things would seem fine. To me, the arguments weren't significant. No one was having an affair; no one was getting beaten.

Since I didn't consider our difficulties to be major, entering couples counseling was an eye-opener. The first day I said, "We have a good marriage and want to learn to make it better." Alix said, "I don't know if we have a good marriage."

The counselor couldn't help us from falling farther into a hole. Yet, I had no idea that Alix considered our marriage at death's door until she filed for divorce. I was used to her threatening to leave me. But for her to actually do it!

The separation was the most emotionally painful time in our lives. The lawyers made it worse. My attorney kept saying, "Close your checking account. Don't give her anything."

Even though I began dating I never stopped loving Alix. I went to an analyst to figure out my role in the breakup. It turned out I hadn't been sensitive to my wife's needs. I couldn't understand why she needed gifts or flowers, or wanted me to call her from work a few times a day. I hadn't had any female role models growing up to show me what girls liked.

Finally, I just couldn't take being separated anymore so, against my lawyer's advice I called Alix and we got back together.

The same arguments started all over again. Alix thinks I walked to get even with her. I left because we were back to where we'd started and I couldn't take it anymore.

We didn't speak for a year. I had a lady friend. But I still loved Alix. Our youngest, a senior in high school, lived part-time with her mother and part-time with me. It was difficult all around.

Alix and I bad-mouthed each other a lot during our time apart. But when I saw her in court a few months after the divorce—well, I just needed us to talk. I wanted her to see that deep inside I'm a sensitive person. I also wanted to let her know that our major problem was both of us being too proud.

We've learned how to communicate in ways that diffuse the tension. Now when Alix says, "I don't like the present you just gave me," I don't jump down her throat, screaming that all she cares about is getting big, expensive gifts. It's about learning to deal with the feelings behind the issue. I ask her why my present is a bust, and repeat or "mirror" back her answer so that we both know I understand it. To Alix, not getting a big gift goes to her insecurities that she's not really important to me.

It's sad to think that throughout our first marriage we had all these avoidable, wrenching arguments. For twenty-four years Alix would complain she wasn't getting her emotional needs met. My response was invariably that she should be happy I wasn't running around at bars.

We remarried on what would have been our twenty-fifth anniversary. This time around our life is truly each other. The kids are gone and we're much more into the marriage than our careers. Before, we had unresolved childhood stuff we wanted the other person to fix. Now Alix is more understanding of the fact that I'm emotionally closed because burying my feelings was how I dealt with my turbulent childhood. And I understand that her father was withholding on both an emotional level and with gifts. These realizations weren't epiphanies. They come slowly, and via great effort.

My advice to couples trying to hold a relationship together: Swallow your pride. That's right—suck it up. Forget the horrible thing your spouse did. Neither of you needs to be right and neither needs to be the dominant party. You just need to love and respect each other.

Sherry Says

If marriage vows reflected the reality that good couples often don't stick together forever, they would go: "To love, honor, and cherish in sickness and in health—until one or both of us gets mad or bored enough to leave."

Alix and Ed learned the hard way that to ensure eternal devotion it is necessary to commit to one another in a way that is much more profound than the legal contract. Paper vows can be broken.

Where Alix Erred

Alix's role in allowing this relationship to bottom out was that she possessed an excess of pride coupled with a dearth of communication skills. It didn't help that she was in denial about how much of what she felt Ed owed her as a husband (great gifts, etc.) stemmed from what she hadn't received from Daddy Dearest.

Then there was her unfortunate habit of threatening to leave whenever the going got rough. When Alix finally followed through on the threat, she owed her husband of twenty-four years a bit more notice than abruptly saying "I'm filing for divorce." If he'd known the marriage was on the line, he would have done anything to remove the rope from around his neck. That "anything" might have resulted in the two of them finding another method of relationship rebuilding besides divorce.

Where Alix Shone

She was attracted to Ed for the right reasons and steadfast in her devotion to home and hearth throughout marriage number one. Plus, she had the gumption to nudge her husband toward therapy in 1985. Too bad she didn't nudge him into switching to a more effective therapist.

Kudos to her for blossoming postdivorce. (*There seemed no need to ever remarry. I had control over my life.*) She didn't return to Ed out of defeat but from a place of strength and self-assurance.

Ingrained habits are extremely difficult to break. It took tremendous will and energy to laboriously learn a new way of communicating with her "old" mate. However once she closed the escape hatch on the relationship, it became sink or swim.

This time around there is no way she is going to drown.

Where Ed Erred

Earth to Ed: Relationships take *work*.

Once the newness of the marriage wore off, he poured all his energy into his career and none into the relationship. Despite agreeing to therapy he made zero effort at seeing Alix's point of view: *I didn't know what an emotional feeling was . . . or much care.*

Although this is the "Erred" section, I'll cut the guy some slack. Since he was so closed off to his own emotions, there was no way he could fathom those of his wife.

Where Ed Shone

During marriage number one he was your basic Boy Scout in a doctor's uniform. A good guy—loyal, dependable, and totally committed to the love of his life. But, like Alix, where he really excelled was in the postdivorce period. He proved himself willing to do whatever it took to not just reunite with his ex, but to make marriage number two stick. Formerly emotion-free, Ed is now comfortable with the language of feelings. He is a self-remade man.

Your Love Lesson From This Couple's Breakup

Many couples who wed young and subsequently crash and burn do so out of a desire to sow their heretofore-unsown wild oats. That wasn't the case here. The only thing Alix and Ed really needed to sow was a better understanding of what made the other tick.

It's evident from their story that a couple who seemingly has everything really has nothing if the primary way they communicate is via arguments punctuated by stubborn lengthy silences.

As Alix and Ed painstakingly demonstrated, it takes a tremendous amount of blood, sweat, and tears to make a marriage work, much less a second marriage to the same partner. Above all, it takes not just uttering the words 'til death do us part, but meaning them in your heart.

Greg & Rachel

Relationship b: 1992; d: 1996

Chapter 7

Don't Mistake Raging Lust for True Love

Greg Says

Rachel was the fourth most serious girlfriend I've ever had. That's including my high school sweetheart who is the mother of my only child. I've never been married and at this rate I might never be.

Unfortunately Rachel's look—thin, no boobs, and short hair—does nothing for me. But the afternoon we met we sat and talked in her apartment and she told me all this heavy stuff about her life. I wanted to heal her. I rubbed her feet then we went into the bathroom and started making out. Rachel's daughter began knocking on the door, shouting, "Mommy, what are you doing in there?"

That night Rachel came over and we lay on my couch swirling our tongues in each other's mouths. The next morning . . . Let's just say I took care of her needs.

In the beginning of the relationship I had my cake and ate it, too. I was dating Rachel and another woman. Sometimes I saw them both twice a day. In basketball that's called a double double, meaning I was scoring a lot!

When Rachel found out about the other woman, she started to break up with me. Instead, I talked her into letting me move into her two-bedroom apartment.

Rachel is a Libra. Her emotions are middle of the road—no extreme highs or lows. She expressed deep anger once by throwing a napkin at me. My take was that if she really loved me she'd passionately fight for me, for *us*.

I want sex all the time. If Rachel was in the apartment, I felt we should be having sex. It bugged me that I always had to be the initiator. I had a wild sexual past and our relationship wasn't naughty enough. I'd say, "Once in a while whisper in my ear when we're out that you don't have panties on."

We set goals for how often we could make love in a given period. Our personal best was having sex over twenty times in one week.

My financial situation was piss-poor: I'd lost all my money in the stock market. So I worked different types of jobs. For a year and a half I had great success as a headhunter. But it didn't last.

I did a lot of "push-pull" behavior with Rachel. When she'd get too close I'd say or do something to push her away. Then I'd pull all the stops out to get her back. I moved in and out of her apartment three separate times. She kept saying, "Why won't you marry me?" I said if she gave me all the sex I wanted, maybe I'd marry her. She never gave me all the sex I wanted and I never proposed.

One of the times we broke up, she followed me to my date's apartment building. I don't know if she heard us having sex or not. I'd also go bananas wondering what guys she was screwing!

During our times apart, she'd use sex to lure me back. Once she let me give her oral sex in a card store. She'd whisper, "If you move in again, I'll do this and that for you." I'd move back and she wouldn't do it.

My theory is she deprived me sexually and I deprived her financially. I admit I was very deficient in the latter area.

I think we helped each other work through a lot of painful stuff. Rachel overcame having suffered sexual abuse. I worked on not letting my fear of abandonment cripple me. I'd suffered so much loss in my life. Everyone I'd loved eventually left. I felt disconnected from everyone but my daughter, and for a while, Rachel.

If Rachel had just gotten it that to me making love meant being in love, things would have worked out between us. If she had sex with me, it meant she felt I was worthy. And since lovemaking was the one thing I did well, I craved every opportunity to show her my love.

I probably don't need as much sex as I say I need. As I come to value myself more I need sex less. But I still like to have it as much as possible. I always will.

Rachel Says

Greg can't be satisfied with one woman. He's sexually insatiable.

Initially I didn't realize this would be a problem. When we met I was twenty-seven and recently divorced from a man twenty years my senior. Greg was thirty-two. He had a head of hair to die for. From the moment we kissed I was a goner.

A mutual friend introduced us because she thought Greg and I might team up to sell a cool new line of nutritional supplements. Greg stopped by for a lunchtime meeting. He stayed the whole afternoon and was so comfortable to talk to that I found myself confiding I'd been sexually abused as a teenager.

He asked me to his place that night for pizza and beer. I stayed over. We did *not* have sex. The next morning when I stepped out of the shower I found a doughnut and coffee waiting for me on the sink.

We slept together for the first time two weeks after we met. I had a four-year-old daughter but found lots of time for Greg. The first six months we were together he drove me *crazy*. We'd have a great date. Then he'd call and say, "I don't want to see you anymore." Around the time Greg finally "cleared the air" and admitted he'd been seeing someone else, his sister died in a car accident. He didn't call for weeks after that tragedy. Eventually he gave in to his feelings for me and we moved in together.

Greg and I experienced these periods of great spiritual and emotional connection where we felt almost like one person. Then he'd pack up and split. This happened six times over the course of our relationship. During one of those periods I asked if he was still seeing the other girl. He denied it but I found out later he was dipping it in two places.

Greg constantly told me I looked like Princess Di. That wasn't a compliment. She wasn't his type! His arrogance extended to the workplace. He was making good money as a recruiter but got fired for taking two-hour lunches. He wound up job-hopping from one waitering gig to another. He had no problem with letting me pay for everything.

In retrospect, I believe his major problem was lack of self-esteem. He felt robbed of many things. His mother abandoned him when he was five; his father remarried a woman who had a son Greg's age. This led to Greg not getting his share of hugs and kisses.

Our relationship wasn't all misery. Greg is one of the funniest people I've ever met. At a restaurant he'd have patrons at nearby tables in stitches with his impressions of famous comics.

Most importantly, Greg was good to my daughter. And he taught me a lot about how to better myself. We read Tony Robbins's books and attended self-improvement seminars together. I went from being an aerobics instructor to a retail-store manager to district manager. Unfortunately Greg couldn't coach himself and stayed mired in self-defeating behaviors.

Why did I stay so long? He's *cute*. And, after enduring a passionless marriage, I'd found a lover who made sex fun, exciting, loving, and romantic! One time he spread rose petals all over the bed before we made love. We did things sexually together we'd never tried with other partners. When the relationship began deteriorating, I clung to how great the sex was . . . at least for me.

Greg wasn't as satisfied. He needed it at least four times a day. He'd constantly claw at me, even in the middle of the night. He couldn't understand why I objected. I told him if he expended as much energy into getting work as he did into lovemaking, he'd be a millionaire. Once I asked him what his top priorities were in a relationship. Communication was number one; numbers two through six were sex!

The final straw was getting evicted from my apartment. This wasn't surprising because Greg was barely contributing to the rent.

A month after we split he asked me to marry him. I was excited and let him move into my new place. But Greg kept putting off the wedding date and he still didn't pay any bills. I got angry and said he had to start forking over some money. He got another waitering job but it was too little too late. We had a fight that was so awful that for the first time in four years I raised my voice and threw things. We were like twelve-year-olds hurling petty accusations. *It's all your fault. No, it's all your fault.*

There are so many things I regret. It was stupid of me to jump so quickly into bed with Greg. Being newly divorced, I craved some excitement. I got hooked on the sex and based the whole relationship around it. I should have made sure that Greg had a good job, and most importantly, that he had good self-esteem. If a person treats himself shabbily, how can he treat his partner any differently?

I'm remarried now and pregnant with another child. Greg's still single, still searching, and still sexually insatiable.

Sherry Says

Love decisions should be based primarily on the inclinations of your head, heart, and gut. While the urgings of your libido should come into play, it shouldn't captain the ship.

Sex had never been fun and easy for Rachel. Thus it was understandable that her lust for Greg (at least temporarily) overtook common sense. And Greg, operating on the assumption that love can only be expressed via genital contact, required a whole lotta lovin'.

Where Greg Erred

Much as I hate lapsing into cliché speak, sometimes it fits. A person must learn to love himself before he can love someone else. The little self-esteem Greg had was tied into sex and affection: *If you love me, you'll sleep with me four times before dinner and three times after dessert.* He needed a bottomless supply of "hugs and kisses" to make up for the ones he didn't get from his nuclear family. Either that, or a course of deep therapy and even deeper introspection.

As Rachel surmised, since he didn't value himself, he couldn't value her. How else to explain his "sins" toward her on the monogamy and monetary fronts? He had no master plan for his life, few life goals other than narcotizing himself as much as possible in a woman's arms.

Where Greg Shone

Despite being one messed-up hombre, Greg managed to give Rachel the push she needed to set career goals and reach them.

Plus, he was a romantic: doughnuts and coffee on the sink, a rose petal–strewn bed. Last but most definitely not least: Until he pushed Rachel beyond the bounds of typical female endurance he knew how to please his woman.

Were Rachel Erred

She forgot that the package should be the *sum* of its parts. Greg cheated on Rachel, sponged off her, couldn't hold down a job, constantly informed his lover that she wasn't his type—yet because he was "cute" Rachel hung in, hoping sex would cure whatever ailed the relationship.

No guy is *that* great a kisser. Sex may be a drug, but it's not a healing one. Temporarily anesthetizing your problems with a feel-good laying on of hands doesn't take the problems away. If life were fair we could indulge in activities that aren't good for us and not suffer morning-after consequences.

In the "not fair" category, Rachel's young daughter, already scarred by divorce, should not have been confronted with Greg as an on-again, off-again roommate. I'm sure from the child's perspective three wasn't company.

What Rachel should have done was draw a line down the middle of a sheet, labeling the halves "Relationship Pluses" and "Relationship Minuses." If the primary plus was great sex— hopefully Rachel would have been forced to realize she wasn't living in the Garden of Eden.

I found it particularly worrisome that after finally kicking Greg to the curb (an event that occurred only after her address became the curb!) she took him back. Not due to actual change on Greg's part, but because she *thought* he uttered the M word.

Where Rachel Shone

She exhibited tenderness and empathy toward the tragedies Greg had suffered and how they had impacted on his psyche. To her, the definition of "man" was not "rock." Greg was allowed to be vulnerable and imperfect.

Rachel was also aware enough about her own imperfections to accept Greg's coaching help. Too bad he didn't coach her how to leave a dysfunctional relationship.

Your Love Lesson From This Couple's Breakup

There were foreboding miscommunications between this couple who played house rather than creating a home together. She recalls his moving into and out of her apartment six times; he said the bag-packing scenario happened but thrice. Most damming, Greg had no recollection of popping the question Rachel insists was posed by his lips.

This dichotomy is sad but unsurprising considering the relationship was based more on what happened between the sheets than between two souls.

My Biggest Heartbreak and What It Taught Me About Love

Dan Elber, 38, choreographer

My biggest heartbreak was not caused from my ex-wife but a woman I dated for six months around fifteen years ago. When we made love it was like our souls touched. Both of us felt we were perfect for each other. But my lover's shrink ultimately convinced her she wasn't ready to have a relationship. When she became ready, she chose to have it with someone other than me.

I responded by descending into a tailspin—the kind where you feel like putting a bag over your head. I went to a bar, pointed to a bottle, and without caring what kind of liquor was in it, held my shot glass out and said, "Fill her up." I kept getting "her" refilled.

I didn't become an alcoholic, but for quite a spell drifted through life not caring much about anything or anyone. My only interest was to wallow in my pain. Then a friend told me, "There are two kinds of pain—the chronic, endless kind and the healing kind that ultimately brings you to a better place."

I started taking small steps to get to that better place—heading out with friends to listen to music instead of drowning myself in the contents of a shot glass. One day I felt myself turn a corner. I realized it had been useful to wallow. Experiencing such intense pain helps you get through the heartbreak quicker than pretending nothing traumatic has happened. But the time for the wallowing kind of pain had passed. I was in the healing stage where the pain was more like an echo rather than ever-present. Life seemed worth living.

Because I did work through the grief of the relationship ending I am now able to be friends with my ex. When I'm in her company, there is no pain and no wishing we could get back together. What's left is a feeling of unity.

Chapter 8

Listen to Your Ego and You Won't Hear Your Heart

Estelle Says

I'm thirty-eight and I've only had two serious relationships in twenty years of dating. My last major love affair ended eleven years ago. Since then, I've had dozens and dozens of romances. Only three lasted over a month.

That's why I made the decision years ago not to put my life on hold waiting for a man. The night I met Paul, I'd gone alone to see a play, then joined two newly married girlfriends for drinks. One of them knew Paul's buddy who was a real hottie! Paul was cute with a nice smile. He kept saying to me, "So you're the single one?"

We understood each other's sensibilities. I'd gone from a high-pressure corporate job to being a performer while Paul had done just the opposite.

He was clearly nervous when we got together for brunch. He

wore a "date outfit"—khaki pants and a woven shirt. It was a Sunday afternoon. He really could have been more casual. At the end of the date he walked me to the subway and blathered about coming to see me do my standup routine. It was obvious he wasn't sure whether or not it would be proper to kiss me.

As I've gotten older my relationships have progressed at a slower pace. I'm nervous when faced with burning passion. I jump in with both feet and get scalded. The slow way is better.

However, Paul was too slow. After five dates he'd barely kissed me. To paraphrase Woody Allen, a relationship has to move forward on the physical level or what you have is a dead shark. This led me to suspect that Paul was gay. C'mon, he'd been a Broadway dancer.

The night I gave Paul the "it's over" talk is the night we wound up sleeping together. From that point on we grew closer. At least I felt we did. Since my tendency is to be a little commitment-phobic, on the rare occasion when I connect with someone emotionally and physically, I do whatever I can to make it last.

Unfortunately there always seems to be some obstacle that keeps me from making love last. One of the first guys I gave my heart to was extremely faithful—but only on the days he saw me. On the days we weren't physically in each other's presence, he was in another woman's pants. It went downhill from there.

It was such a relief to meet a nice guy like Paul. In this case the obstacle to lasting love was his hope that one day I'd wake up and have Jesus in my heart. There was more of a chance of my winning the lottery—I don't play!—than my suddenly embracing the Son of God. It didn't help that Paul had been divorced for just six months. So many of our conversations revolved around "my ex, my ex, my ex."

Once we made love, though, I was hooked. I had a weeklong comedy gig in Myrtle Beach and made the mistake of telling Paul

I missed him terribly. That freaked him out. And it freaked me out that immediately after sex he'd invariably have one foot in his jeans.

I told Paul we had to end the sexual part of our friendship. He agreed but when we'd get together he'd try to have sex! That's a man for you.

Still, Paul wrote a new blueprint for how I now expect to be treated by men. He was unfailingly kind, supportive, and respectful. If I had a hard day, he'd come over and give me a one-hour foot massage.

BP (Before Paul) my boyfriends routinely did crappy things like stand me up and hit on other women in front of me. The worse they'd act, the more I'd grovel to keep their attention. I'd buy these jerks gifts and cook them candlelit-dinners.

The therapist I've been seeing for fifteen years thinks my attraction to abusive people is a replication of my childhood relationship with my sister. She treated me like gum on her shoe. Partly due to seeing at last how nice it is to be treated nicely, I won't be gum under a guy's shoe anymore.

It was so exciting to be attracted to someone nice that I ignored all the divisive issues between Paul and me: Religion; his ex-wife hang-up. At my age, to spend four months in a relationship that can't go anywhere isn't smart or healthy.

I went through a lot of pain over Paul. It's not that he was the one, but he was the closest I've come in a long time. When you get that close, it reminds you of what you don't have.

Paul Says

I found it easier to become a dancer on Broadway than to forge a healthy love relationship. My five-year marriage eroded because my wife and I couldn't communicate. Actually, Jane communicated to me loud and clear when she had an affair.

Estelle and I met a year after my divorce. By then I was thirty-two and had left show business to work in graphic design. Instead of dating other dancers whose primary focus was their careers, I was meeting women who grilled me: Did I make $100,000? Did I have a 401(k)? Suddenly there were all these standards I had to pass before a girl would sleep with me. I understood. It's not that women don't want to work. They need to feel their man cares enough to be *willing* to take care of them.

It was nice, though, that Estelle didn't ask me any of these questions. We met in a bar. Her two girlfriends started talking to me. That broke the ice. Estelle's friends were married so that narrowed my options about which one to pursue.

Our first date was a Sunday brunch, then a walk through a flea market. It went well so I asked her out again. I'd been running across girls who would dump me after the first date. I believe the problem was my not being a bad guy. I was a good boy aspiring to be a rebel without a cause. To that end, sometimes I don't shave. Estelle didn't seem to mind my essential decency as a human being.

Maybe I was too decent for her. Because I didn't immediately put on the moves, she assumed I was gay. What happened was that she took great, great offense because I stopped her in the middle of performing fellatio on me. She believes this is one of her great skills. But I didn't know her that well, we hadn't had intercourse yet, I prefer looking at someone's face . . . so I pushed her away. She said very clinically, "I told my girlfriends that I thought you might be gay. Have you ever been with a man?" I was so offended. I felt like hurling an epithet and walking out the door but I needed to set the story straight.

Looking back at that night I still ask myself why I didn't charge out that door. Although I'm comfortable with my sexuality I fear what other people think. I felt this primal urge to prove my manhood by throwing Estelle down and taking her. We wound up making out. I thought she was a wacko but there I was letting her kiss me. . . .

A few nights later, Valentine's Day, Estelle broke up with me at one of the most romantic restaurants in New York. She's Jewish and was hung up on my being a born-again Christian. Initially I wasn't too happy to be dumped. Particularly since I had just bought her dinner. After a few minutes I felt relieved. So did she. Now that it was on the table that we didn't expect anything other than friendship from the other, we raced to her apartment and finally had intercourse.

The truth was that although I felt a physical attraction to Estelle, when I looked at her Cupid wasn't shooting arrows over my head.

We embarked on what I thought was a sexual friendship. Estelle said she was fine with the way things were, then would make snide comments like how I had one leg in my jeans before we even finished making love. I kept thinking, "She wants a relationship. I don't."

We started fighting. There was a lot of tension and bad feeling. I knew Estelle hadn't always had great luck with men. I didn't want to be another guy who treated her badly. This may sound conceited but I decided to rescue Estelle from me. I broke up with her, this time for real.

It was a bit rough making the transition to friendship. One time Estelle said, "You want to kiss me right now, don't you?" I didn't but that was obviously what she needed to believe at that point.

My relationship with Estelle broke a lot of negative patterns for me. She's very passionate and communicative—firsts for me. My wife was neither. Yet, I'm afraid I'm looking for a mirror image of my ex. If that's not sick enough I slept with Estelle not because of her great qualities but to assert my maleness. Maybe I'm not such a nice guy after all.

Sherry Says

One needn't be a psychic to predict that a man who enters into a sexual liaison based not on the dictates of his heart and (big or little) head, but of his ego, is destined to cause confusion and pain.

Where Estelle Erred

It is a tragedy that it took twenty years of dating for Estelle to find a guy who didn't treat her like gum under his shoe. There is serious pathology at play (I suspect beyond duplicating a dysfunctional sibling dance) that keeps her emotionally wedded to men incapable of participating in a mature, caring relationship.

Recently, Estelle made big changes on the professional front to forge a more fulfilling career. Her first-ever alliance with a nice guy is a sign she's finally ready to do the work necessary to achieve healthy, lasting love. A step toward achieving that goal might be to ferret out a shrink who can nudge her toward speedier insights.

Once Estelle finds a potential keeper, hopefully she will treat him with more tact than she demonstrated toward poor Paul. *I told my girlfriends that I thought you might be gay. Have you ever been with a man?* Ouch, and double ouch. It was one thing to air her suspicions about his sexual proclivities, another to admit she'd shared them with friends!

Estelle was too honest with Paul but not honest enough with herself. She knew he wasn't "the one" for a variety of reasons: religious differences, his continuing passion for his ex, and lack of passion for her. She also knew that having sex would hook her. Yet, like so many women since Eve, she bit into the oh-so-tempting fruit. Like the garden dweller, Estelle got less than peachy results.

Where Estelle Shone

Kudos to Estelle for not putting her life on hold while waiting for *the* man to show up. And, just as Paul showed Estelle another side of the male species, she proved to her lover that not all women were cold, passionless cheaters. He now knows that at least one female possesses humor and heart.

Where Paul Erred

Although essentially a man with morals, when Paul fell off the nice-guy wagon he landed with a heart-hurting thud. Only the heart he hurt wasn't his own.

I thought she was a wacko yet there I was letting her kiss me. While his need to prove his masculinity to Estelle after her passion-reducing jab was understandable it was also irresponsible. Once he started sleeping with Estelle, his conflicts about having a sexual relationship with someone he didn't love led him to treat her insensitively. "Afterplay" does not mean immediately hopscotching into your pants to bolt out the door.

It was unwise of him to immediately throw himself into dating postdivorce. He should have first taken time to assess the psychological damage wrought by a dysfunctional marriage. Paul won't cease looking for a mirror image of his ex until he is ready to truly reflect on why he stayed for so long in a relationship that offered neither passion nor communication.

Where Paul Shone

Although there is controversy over whether he or Estelle ultimately ended the sexual part of their friendship, Paul definitely attempted to be clear throughout the liaison that his interest in her was not of a serious nature.

It's impossible to come down too hard on a guy who offers hour-long foot massages to a woman who has had a rough day.

Your Love Lesson From This Couple's Breakup

Once again, the accounts of an ex-couple differ on several pertinent points. Estelle says Paul was divorced six months when they met; he insists it was one year. Each believes he or she delivered the final coup de grâce to the "sexual friendship." Each cites different reasons for the demise of the relationship: Estelle believes the religious divide was a major factor while Paul would say under oath that his lukewarm romantic feelings toward her undid their relationship. As they uncoupled, Estelle accused Paul of still trying to have sex. He felt that that's her womanly ego talking.

Now that we're on the subject: These two wouldn't have been a couple beyond their first five dates if not for Paul's too-healthy ego.

Buddhist leader Sogyal Rinpoche defined ego as "garrulous, demanding, hysterical, calculating . . ." In all matters, but particularly in those of the heart, to give the directives of your ego more credence than the wise inner guide struggling to be heard is a dangerous pastime. Paul listened to the self-involved screed: *I must prove to this person that I am a stud even if she is not the woman I seek.* He subsequently acted against his and Estelle's best interests.

The more you can recognize and ignore the ego rants bubbling within you, the more you will get in touch with that still voice of wisdom that can help lead you to real love.

Chapter 9

Don't Treat Your Lover Like an Afterthought

Michael Says

I still can't put my finger on what went wrong. I thought Jan was the soul mate I'd been waiting for my entire twenty-four years on the planet. I thought I could have with her what my dad has with my mom—a cosmic connection.

Jan and I met through my job. I spent a lot of time as a consultant traveling from university to university teaching fraternity chapters how to throw safe parties. While on the road, I went to a student bash and there was this beautiful twenty-one-year-old—Jan.

I was enmeshed in a dysfunctional relationship back home so I wasn't looking for romantic entanglements. But Jan and I really clicked. We slept together the first night. There were no inhibitions on either side. It felt comfortable to tell each other everything about our past relationships and deepest secrets. . . . Plus, we had *extremely* weird things in common. Both of us had tattoos to commemorate the death of a loved one who had OD'd on heroin.

I flew home and broke up with my girlfriend. Then Jan and I continued getting to know each other long distance. One weekend I paid her airfare to visit me. A few weeks later I went back east for her college graduation.

After seeing each other just five times, we decided to spend the summer backpacking through Europe. Yes, it was difficult being together 24/7 but we came back still a couple.

I'd said "I love you" to girlfriends past, but before Jan I didn't know what the word meant. I never wanted to be apart from her. I could tell her anything. I had absolutely no desire to cheat on her. We were never critical of each other, at least not during the first year.

Our second summer together things started falling apart. Jan started putting me in the background of her life. Here is a direct quote from my other half: "My priority will be spending every weekend at my parents' beach house. You're welcome to join me if you like." That really hurt. To no avail, I'd beg, "Can't you give me one weekend?"

The weekends I did go to the beach house I'd notice Jan's ex-boyfriend hanging all over her. I knew Jan wasn't interested yet she did nothing to shoot him down. Since I don't handle it real well when a guy is hitting on the woman I love *I* spoke to him. She got upset with me for hurting *his* feelings.

Nothing I did was good enough—not the way I dressed, or cut my hair. Here's an example: I was accompanying Jan to a black tie wedding. I bought five dress shirts for her inspection—she nixed *all* of them.

Instead of dealing with stressful issues in her life—a scary medical checkup or an unfulfilling job—she lashed out at me. Early on, Jan and I could talk about everything. Suddenly the opposite was true. We couldn't muster up the strength to try to resolve our problems. Sweeping them under the rug only increased the tension between us.

Jan and I stopped trying. Simple as that. Love shouldn't be so much work. I made the ultimate decision to break up. We were driving to yet another wedding and she kept laying into me. I said, "That's it. When we get back to your house tonight, I'm leaving. We're done."

I stuck to my guns. I loved her to death but she wasn't acting like she cared about me. I'd put so much into the relationship. I moved cross country to be closer to her, constantly gave her fun presents, and did anything I could to make her happy. In return I got, "My priority will be spending every weekend at my parents' beach house."

If things had gone differently, come the fall I'd have asked her to move in with me. Instead, when the summer ended, so did we.

Jan Says

I don't know exactly what love is. Yet I know that's what I feel for Michael. I've learned more about myself in the first six weeks after our breakup than in my whole life previous. I've learned enough to say that nearly everything that went wrong between us was my fault.

Michael was my third serious boyfriend, but my first adult relationship. He's a great guy—extremely caring, incredibly thoughtful, and easy to love.

He *lives* to love. He showers the woman in his life with affection and attention. He'd walk into my house, pick me up, and twirl me around—basking in our togetherness. That sort of display was shocking to me. Expressiveness makes me nervous. I'm realizing that I'm like my mom, and that's scary. She's cold. She's more than cold. She's the ultimate ball-buster. She cows my dad. Mom shows love by cracking sarcastic jokes. I worked so hard to earn her love but I never felt it.

Michael kept asking me to show him my love. I wanted the opposite from him. I wanted Michael to turn it off. I asked him to stop stuffing my mailbox with gifts. Then, for my birthday he gave me a diamond necklace. My "thank you" was a peck on the cheek. He wanted a bigger reaction but that was the best I could do.

It was unfair of Michael not to realize how important my parents' beach house is to me. They only rent the house for eight weeks a year and it's my favorite place in the world. Besides, Michael was beyond welcome to visit whenever he wanted.

Why didn't I tell my high school boyfriend to stop treating me like his girlfriend? I didn't want to lead him on but I hate confrontation. Unfortunately I didn't have trouble ripping into Michael when he talked to my ex.

Michael kept pushing against my barriers. He wanted me to be more like him. I was comfortable being who I was, and unhappy that who I was couldn't make him happy. I wish now with all my heart that I'd been more attentive to his needs instead of turning into my mom. I shut down and we fell apart. We stopped talking, having fun, or making love.

There was no specific breakup incident. I thought we were just taking a hiatus from the relationship. We started casually dating simultaneously. Today Michael told me he's ready to get serious with someone. That is *killing* me. He is sweeping this girl off her feet just like he did with me. Only she appreciates his gestures.

Before the breakup all my emotions were dammed up. Now they're gushing out in a torrential flood. I'm realizing that I have to change the way I relate to other people or I'll be alone forever. I went on three dates with a guy who told me I'm incredibly hard to read, that I gave him zero feedback about my reactions to him. He didn't understand why I'm so thick.

That pretty much says it. My thickness cost me the greatest guy in the world.

Sherry Says

Unlike the little engine that could, this couple could not. Instead of doing anything and everything to pull themselves over a seemingly impassable obstacle to the other side, Jan and Michael let their relationship simply stall in its tracks.

Michael called Jan his *soul mate* while she referred to her ex as *the greatest guy in the world*. Yet, at the first hint of an impediment in the path of true love both gave up. They put other things (i.e., a beach house, inability to easily communicate, pride) before each other and that became all she wrote for a relationship that could easily have kept on chugging.

Where Michael Erred

His obsessive search for a "cosmic" connection that emulates the one between his parents led Michael to act precipitously. His love style is to leapfrog from relationship to relationship. (He was still *in* one when he met Jan.) When one crashes and burns, instead of taking time out for a period of reflection, regrets, and renewal, he saddles up at the next barn.

Once "saddled," his rash behavior continues. Rather than slowly getting to know his new love object or whether she truly suits him, Michael instantly showers her with copious amounts of affection and attention. He's willing to go all out for passion: buy diamond necklaces, relocate. It's difficult for him to understand why his partner won't immediately do the same. My philosophy: You've got to present gifts for the joy of giving, not for the expectation of what you'll receive in return.

While love doesn't mean *never saying you're sorry*, it does mean *never trying to change your partner's personality*. Michael couldn't accept that Jan's lack of expressiveness was part of her makeup, not proof that she didn't love him enough. So he committed cardinal relationship sin number 344 and tried to turn Jan into someone she wasn't—a female Michael.

When that effort failed and Jan withdrew into a shell, he withdrew into one of his own. After he finally cried uncle and said we're done, he immediately leapfrogged into a new woman's arms.

Where Michael Shone

In many respects, he is a woman's fantasy come to life: a man whose reason for living is to bestow on his beloved presents both material and ethereal.

Michael is basically a good guy and a great boyfriend—supportive, tender, passionate, and eager to please (e.g., buying five dress shirts for milady's inspection).

Although he could have chugged a lot harder to make this relationship work, it's hard to quibble with his need to feel like he was his partner's priority.

Where Jan Erred

Jan is learning the hard way that not all the changes love brings are desired ones. She quickly embraced certain character traits possessed by her lover such as fidelity, passion, and a sunny nature. She cringed, however, when faced with Michael's love of giving elaborate love tokens. The correct response to a boyfriend's gift is not to transmit the message: "Return to sender."

Jan couldn't see that Michael's extravagance was partially due to his need to receive assurances of her love. She assumed all she needed to do to maintain Michael's devotion into infinity was show up. The definition of *not taking a lover for granted* translates into treating said lover with *at least* the same amount of respect and compassion as you bestow on an ex. And to never, ever utter to your partner the phrase, "A beach house is my priority over you."

To avoid treating future boyfriends with such callousness, Jan must go from a myopic view of love (*What do I want my man to do for me?*) to one that encompasses another person's needs (*How can we make each other happy without compromising our personalities?*).

Happily, Jan is beginning to understand why she made these elemental relationship mistakes.

Where Jan Shone

It is unfortunate that her best moves in the relationship have been made postbreakup. She is bravely delving into her psyche to discern the reasons for her "thickness." In this case, blaming mom isn't a total cop-out.

Once Jan moves from her current phase of totally assailing herself for the relationship's demise, she will hopefully become clear-sighted enough to determine if she truly wants to change major character traits. Her emotional restraint is not necessarily a weakness as long as it's accompanied by an ability to make her lover feel loved.

Yes, she must learn the importance of the two Cs: communication and compromise. But her perfect mate might ultimately prove to be a man less overtly demonstrative than Michael.

Your Love Lesson From This Couple's Breakup

Most of us lack a beach house that is our favorite place in the world. But who hasn't been tempted to put something ephemeral ahead of a partner? If you truly love someone and are in the relationship for the long haul, don't give in to that temptation. You can't have it all—at least not all the time.

Not fully convinced? Which is more fun as a cuddle partner: a beach house or a body?

My Biggest Heartbreak and What It Taught Me About Love

Lin Sutherland, late 40s, writer

I was with Dave from age eighteen to twenty-eight. He was an artist and the love of my life. We had a great relationship, the kind you can have only when both of you are young, not yet battle-scarred, and completely bonded. The breakup was my fault. I got distracted and allowed myself to take Dave for granted.

We lived in Hollywood and I got an opportunity to make a movie with a big Hollywood director. Only it was clear I wouldn't actually get to do the movie unless I slept with this director. So I did.

If only I'd stepped back and looked at the ramifications of what I was doing and faced that it could do permanent damage to Dave and me. He was devastated and left immediately. Two years later guilt still tore at me and I asked Dave if we could get together to talk. By then he was married to my former best friend. Oh yes, she snapped him up the second he was on the market.

Dave and I met in a park near where we used to live. I asked if he could forgive me. He was gracious and generous and said, "Of course, Lin. Life goes on." He made it okay for me to forgive myself.

I have never again forgotten that the most important thing in life is to be loyal to the things you believe in and the people you love. Faithfulness is a part of loyalty. The movie got made, was well received at Sundance and won a bunch of awards. It launched an eleven-year career for me in Hollywood. Yet this "success" occurred at too great a cost.

Stacey & Thomas
Relationship b: 1993; d: 1999

Chapter 10

Getting Married Is No Cure for a Troubled Relationship

Stacey Says

The night I met Thomas is a drunken blur. It was a few weeks after my twenty-second birthday. I had just moved out west. A few girlfriends and I were hanging out at a bar. Thomas was bartending. He made us *killer* shots. My friend Colleen and I did forward rolls and cartwheels into the laps of the patrons. Colleen and Thomas hooked up that night and he stayed over at our apartment. They were too out of it for anything to happen.

Colleen had a boyfriend so Thomas and I started dating. I'd had a slew of guys all through high school and college but never found one who made me want to stop sleeping around. I met Thomas and thought, "Oh my God, this is *the* guy!"

For the first few months after Thomas and I hooked up, I was also dating my boss. He was a very wealthy nightclub owner who'd buy me gifts and take me on fabulous trips. One time

Thomas asked me where I'd been all weekend. I made up some story but Greg had taken me to Spain.

Eventually Thomas said, "You can't have Greg and me. Choose." I was too chicken to tell Greg it was over. I just stood him up for a date.

Things were great between Thomas and me while we were in Colorado. Our second summer together we went east and crashed at my parents' house. Thomas got a job at a software company that turned out to be a nightmare. But he kept lecturing me that I should use my college degree to find an accounting gig. I'd been making tons of money bartending. I had no idea what I wanted to do with my life, but I sure wasn't ready for an office job.

Thomas and I went backpacking in Europe for a few weeks. Basically we had a great time but one night Thomas got really drunk and said mean things: *we needed to split up; he didn't know if he loved me* . . . I cried the entire night. The next morning Thomas said he'd been kidding!

After that trip we moved back out west to waiter and bartend at a friend's restaurant. It was fun but eventually I got tired of that lifestyle and began wanting to do something with a future. I took an accounting job at a hotel. Thomas stayed at the restaurant. His head was now thoroughly into the party scene and he wasn't supportive of my new direction.

Basically, he hated that I didn't depend on him as much. What matters most to Thomas is being someone else's entire world. I came from a large, loving family. Thomas was an only child and had never learned how to compromise or share. When we were out with friends, he'd be angry if I "stole" the limelight. I learned to suck it up and let him be the star.

His inconsiderate nature became a huge problem. I did all the cleaning. Thomas would come in—kick everything around to find what he wanted, then rush out, leaving a huge mess. If I asked him to do anything domestic, he'd accuse me of nagging. Lots of times he called me a bitch. Nothing I did or said was ever right.

Throughout most of our six years together I loved doing nice things for Thomas. I'd surprise him with a kayak just because it would make him happy. The point at which the relationship ended for me for was when I lost the desire to do things for him *just because*. As I came to that realization Thomas shocked me out of my shoes by proposing. We'd been together for five years and I loved him so my answer was yes.

In the back of my mind I had lots of doubts. Two weeks before the ceremony I asked Thomas, "Are we doing the right thing?" He said, "I'll do anything in the world for you. I promise."

We had a huge wedding on Memorial Day weekend, 1999. Our family and friends flew in from around the country to attend.

Thomas freaked out about a week later. He said, "Oh my God. I shouldn't have married you. I can't give you all the attention you want."

What I wanted was for him to be a normal husband—to tell me he loved me and that I was beautiful. Other guys made comments that made me feel better about myself; Thomas constantly belittled me. He didn't look at me with an expression that breathed, "You're the one."

Things got progressively worse. There were days I'd work twenty-four hours in a row, sleep six, and start all over again. I was insane with stress. Thomas couldn't have cared less. He'd just gotten a job in real estate and that's all he talked about. He actually told me that with our money troubles that I should consider working more hours!

Plus, he was flirting with every skirt in sight. He'd always had an eye for the women but this seemed like spite, a way to get back at me for not being available to him 24/7.

One weekend I snapped. I walked to a girlfriend's house and said, "I can't do it anymore."

I don't blame Thomas for driving me to leave. He had a lot of family issues with his mom he couldn't work through that left him selfish, scared, and bitter.

Throughout our relationship Thomas accused me of sleeping around. He's convinced I cheated on him with Sam, who is now my fiancé. It's not true. I hung out with Sam while Thomas and I were together, but that's all. And who is Thomas to talk? During our engagement, I witnessed him sucking on a girl's toes at a bar.

I still miss Thomas. The day our divorce was final I felt like I'd lost my best friend. But the person you love should make you feel good about yourself, not incompetent and small. From the moment I wake up until I put my head on the pillow, Sam makes me feel like the most special human being he's ever met.

Thomas Says

Besides my mother, Stacey was the first woman who wormed an "I love you" out of me. Given that mom abandoned me when I was twelve, I found it hard to trust a female enough to say that phrase.

My mother didn't *literally* abandon me. I was an only child. Growing up, Dad was never around so Mom and I became best friends. Then my parents split and Mom moved in with this guy who didn't want me around. I said to her, "It's the ugly boyfriend or me." The upshot was I moved in with my dad.

Throughout my teens and early twenties I cut a wide swath through many girls. At twenty-five I met Stacey and something clicked. I recognized parts of myself in her. We were a great team. She and I liked the same things: drinking and partying. From the get-go, though, Stacey wasn't trustworthy. Whenever she'd preface a story with honestly, I'd think, *Oh, the* last *time we talked about this you lied*. Stacey said her relationship with Greg was strictly friendship. Then why would she spend the night at his house? Her boss had money while I could barely afford to take Stacey out for a hamburger.

My insecurities and distrust continued throughout the relationship. I built a cast-iron plate around my heart. This distancing device caused me to say things to Stacey like, "I don't know if I love you." These statements protected me but hurt her.

I come from my dad's mold of tough-cut men who don't express feelings or admit we're hurt. Stacey would constantly be at me for compliments. Yes, she was—is—incredibly beautiful and intelligent. Why is it my responsibility to make her feel good about herself?

It was amazing to watch Stacey's metamorphosis through the years from bartender to accountant who won the title "Employee of the Month." I tried my best to be supportive and helpful. I'd brag to all our friends how proud I was of her success.

When I got a sales manager job at the hotel where Stacey worked, she got upset—like I was horning in on her domain. It especially irked her that I started out at a higher salary level.

Things at home were tense, too. I'm not the cleanest guy in the world but nothing I did was good enough. If I took the trash out, she'd be at me that I didn't put a new bag in the garbage can. I'd wash the dishes and get reamed for not drying them properly. When nothing you do for the other person is good enough, you stop wanting to do anything. I finally said, "If you really don't think I do anything around here, I'll stop." I stopped.

I still loved her, still thought we were a great team, so five years after we hooked up I surprised her with an engagement ring. Stacey didn't say anything, but I knew she was disappointed the band was gold, not silver.

During our engagement she got drunk and had sex with one of my good friends. Stacey and I are both big flirts but the difference is I would never take it anywhere. Stacey denied to me that she'd had sex with Bill. Then she admitted everything to a mutual friend. This friend spilled the truth to me after Stacey and I finally split. To this day Stacey denies she had sex with Bill. Whether she did or didn't, the intent was there and I consider that a huge betrayal.

Our wedding was the happiest day of my life. All our friends watched Stacey and me unite in love.

Sliding a wedding ring onto Stacey's finger broke the cast-iron plate around my heart. My ability to love and be loved reached a whole new level. My emotions toward my wife became spiritual in nature. I was ready for us to have a true union.

Stacey went the opposite way. Her frustrations with me grew. A few weeks before the wedding she had told me all the ways she needed me to be different. I said I'd try. I did try but after thirty-one years of being a strong, silent type, it's hard to instantly change your nature. Stacey didn't give me a fair shot.

The first time I noticed Stacey not wearing her wedding band happened a month after the wedding. One night she didn't come home 'til 4 A.M. She said she was watching videos with her friend Betty. When I asked Betty later if she and Stacey had had a fun girls' night, Betty said, "Huh? I wasn't with Stacey."

The next time I noticed her ring on our nightstand was the weekend she spent in Grand Junction camping out and watching a dirt bike race with this guy Sam and around twenty other people. I was stuck at home 'cause of work. Later I asked friends who'd supposedly been at the race if it was as big a blast as Stacey said it was. I found out Sam and Stacey were the only ones who'd gone to Grand Junction.

I moved out that night. Stacey came home while I was packing and cried that we could work things out. She denied having sex with Sam. I didn't want to be lied to anymore, so I took off.

A week later we had lunch at a Mexican joint in town and she asked how to fix things. I said, "Stop seeing Sam." The two of them went away together that weekend. That told me all I needed to know.

We're divorced now. I still hear from her periodically, "Thomas, I love you. Sam isn't who I want." She's *such* a good liar.

There are lots of things I did wrong that contributed to her cheating on me. But there are also lots of things I did that Stacey never gave me credit for. She has reasons in her head why our relationship broke down, and those reasons revolve around my many screw-ups.

Toward the end we had enormous money pressures and were both working a bunch of different jobs. Yet after we split Stacey said she contributed *all* the income. I pointed out how that wasn't true and I outlined exactly who made how much from which gig. She said, "Oh, right."

I adore Stacey but I could never take her back. Trust has been breached. Yet I now understand that if you love a woman you have to give up parts of your soul to her. It's imperative to open your heart fully and give your lover what she says she needs.

If I could turn back the clock this time around I would worship Stacey.

Punch/Counterpunch

STACEY: Thomas bought me a gold wedding band when he knew I only liked silver! How's that for not paying attention to my desires?

THOMAS: I should have known the marriage vows didn't mean much to her when she wouldn't even wear her wedding ring.

THOMAS: Stacey can't stop cheating or lying. She slept with one of my best friends during our engagement, then denied it. She slept with Sam before our marriage broke up, and denied that too.

STACEY: Okay, I slept with Bill during the engagement, but only because Thomas was never around. Bill was more like my boyfriend than Thomas. And it only happened one time out of pure camaraderie. It was no big deal—that's why I didn't tell Thomas. If I'd slept with Sam before Thomas moved out— I didn't!—that would have been a big deal. Because by then I was already half in love with Sam—and half out of love with Thomas.

STACEY: The job had been the one place where I wasn't "Thomas and Stacey", just Stacey. Thomas is so big and overbearing when he enters a room he just takes over.

THOMAS: My getting a job at her workplace got Stacey ridiculously bent out of shape.

Sherry Says

After living together for half a decade, Thomas and Stacey's love affair derailed after scarcely one month of marriage. By the time of the ceremony, if the troubled relationship wasn't dead it was certainly on life support. The couple was no longer putting much effort into making each other happy. For them, saying marital vows was the romantic equivalent of a Hail Mary pass. In the end, they dropped the ball.

Where Stacey Erred

Her emotions and passions are close to the surface—sometimes too close. Stacey takes what (whom) she wants, and damn the consequences. An example of this pattern at work: Stacey falling in love with Thomas practically at first sight yet continuing to sleep with her older, wealthier boss. Sadly, her pattern for extricating herself from self-created messes resembled a puppy skedaddling from the scene of the crime. *I was too chicken to tell Greg it was over. I just stood him up for a date.*

One of the modes of communication utilized by Stacey was nagging. The way to get a man to do domestic chores is not to lambaste his efforts but positively reinforce his attempts.

Another "tool" in her communication kit arsenal was lying. She denied to Thomas that she was sleeping with her older, wealthier boss. Years later Stacey swore she hadn't slept with Bill. As to whether she had sex with Sam before officially breaking up with Thomas: Draw your own conclusions.

Because Thomas couldn't deliver the verbal assurances she craved, Stacey frequently assumed the worst of him. She *refused* to believe that Thomas was proud rather than threatened by her transformation from party girl to employee of the month.

If her doubts about the relationship were so pervasive, she should have insisted Thomas join her in couples counseling instead of holy matrimony. In her heart of hearts, does she truly believe she gave Thomas a fair shot to change inbred character traits that irritated her?

Was this randy, fun-loving young thing truly ready to settle into a monogamous union? That's a question she's got to answer for herself. Even Stacey would have to agree that it is not proper form to celebrate your one month wedding anniversary by going camping with another man.

Where Stacey Shone

She has a good heart and genuinely wanted to "do nice things" for her husband during the bulk of their relationship. She exhibited great understanding of how Thomas's family background had crippled his ability to have a nurturing, caring relationship with a woman.

Stacey has the self-awareness to realize that she needs the man in her life to make her feel like the most special human being on earth. Hopefully, she is coming to realize she in turn should make her lover feel the same way.

Where Thomas Erred

It is understandable why Thomas erected a cast-iron plate around his heart. However, keeping Stacey at an emotional remove was the surest way to ultimately lose her. Thomas tried to give Stacey a gruff "tough-love" style of emotional support despite her repeated assertions that she needed to hear soft, pretty words.

When Thomas moved in with Stacey, this only child was a master at the art of self-absorption and a stranger to the necessity of compromise and selfless deeds within a relationship. He frequently displayed insensitivity (suggesting his exhausted partner work more hours when she was already toiling round the clock) and a misplaced macho bravado (deciding if his domestic attempts weren't good enough, he'd simply stop making them).

Around the time Thomas shut down emotionally, he also popped the question. The query he should have made was to himself: "If I can't trust Stacey and we can't communicate, might therapy help us save our relationship?"

His deepest, darkest fear was that a woman would betray and abandon him just like mama. Did he create a self-fulfilling prophecy by choosing a partner who he believed couldn't keep her zipper up? For those without a scorecard: Stacey's conquests were Greg, Bill, Sam. . . . Thomas used these apparent betrayals to fuel the distrust and distance he felt toward Stacey.

And did this self-confessed flirt truly *never take it anywhere* with another woman?

Where Thomas Shone

It was a leap of faith for someone so emotionally damaged to give his heart to one woman. Thomas used all his relationship skills to make the relationship work—unfortunately those skills, at least initially, weren't very practiced or effective.

But he proved able to change. Toward the end of their relationship, Thomas really put himself on the line and pledged to Stacey an eagerness to do *anything* to forge a true union of souls. Regardless of the outcome, he's richer as a human being for having made the effort. Witness his willingness to accept culpability for partially driving Stacey into Sam's arms. Although he now realizes he didn't appreciate his wife enough when they were together, he also realizes it would be foolhardy to reunite with a woman he can't trust.

Here's hoping Thomas can eventually allow another woman to pierce the rebuilt iron plate around his heart.

Your Love Lesson From This Couple's Breakup

Thomas and Stacey genuinely loved each other. However, the relationship suffered from their immaturity and emotional guardedness. Their communication styles were polar opposites: gruff versus emotional. This chasm created even more impetus for hurt feelings, misinterpretations, and lassitude. Both reached the point of assuming the other untrustworthy and incapable of change. Each was invested in being right rather than in acknowledging the validity of the other's point of view.

When the pair couldn't connect they should have opted either to break up or to get help learning communication skills. Instead they chose the sure-to-fail approach and made a desperate attempt to patch up the leaky holes in their love boat with a piece of paper: a marriage license.

Dan & Cindy

Relationship b: 1995; d: 1996

Chapter 11

Don't Assume the Two of You Are on the Same Romantic Wavelength

Dan Says

The eight months I spent with Cindy marked my first semi-serious relationship in six years. I had a quickie "practice" marriage with my college sweetheart, and a longer, more intense one during my thirties that broke up because we lived on separate ends of the country.

My work in television had required me to move three times in five years. By the time I relocated to Utah I was forty-five, ready to settle down in one place, and be with one good woman.

The first date with Cindy was one of those where you talk until 3:00 o'clock in the morning. I couldn't wait to see her again. We wound up having four dates in the span of five days. We spent the night together at the end of our third date.

Our first few weeks were very intense—we spent most of our free time together. I took her to a family wedding and Cindy strode into this roomful of strangers like she owned the town.

I fell harder and harder for this fun, fearless, adventurous woman. Then Cindy informed me she was dating another man. Eventually it came out that he was one of my reporters. Joe cared more about his job than Cindy, so he bowed out gracefully . . . a gesture I appreciated.

I still thought Cindy was wonderful. At that point there had been no commitment between us so I had no reason to feel upset that she'd been dating someone else.

After we passed over the Joe speed bump, things progressed beautifully. We continued spending most of our spare time together. Communication between us was good and sex was *wonderful*. . . . We had lots of fun together and seemed to share common goals. Around six months into the relationship, in a roundabout way I asked her to move in with me.

Cindy and a friend were helping me house hunt. I made a crack to the friend that I might need to look at bigger places because I hoped I'd have a roommate.

When Cindy heard about my crack she freaked out. We hadn't talked about the level of our commitment but it had seemed clear to me we were on the same track. I quickly discovered in Cindy's mind what she and I shared wasn't serious at all.

We had a huge fight. She gave me the "maybe we shouldn't date each other" speech and stopped seeing me for a week or so.

I started bumping into a lot of Cindy's ex-boyfriends. I discovered that her relationship pattern was to date someone for five months, then kaput. I also realized that Cindy kept me at arm's length. She'd talk about things in her distant past but nothing at all recent. And she *rarely* spoke about her feelings.

It gradually crystallized for me that we were on different wavelengths. I held out some hope until she did something—well, crappy. We were still sort of dating. One night I was hanging out at her place. She got a call from a new beau and took off, leaving me with cold pizza and a broken heart. Her truly reprehensible behavior was what I needed to knock me back into my senses. No matter how much I wished it wasn't so, Cindy didn't know how to conduct a relationship, at least none I'd want to be a part of.

I gave Cindy the "I don't want to be your friend" speech. She became very upset, having had no clue that what she'd done might have hurt me. Her attitude hadn't been malicious, just unaware: "I'm out for a good time and if a guy falls in love with me, that's his problem."

This episode was a turning point for Cindy as well. I persuaded her to go into therapy to look at why she thought all men were assholes.

I had loved Cindy. Trite as it sounds she was one of the few women I've ever met who could light up a room just by walking into it. From the pizza incident on we became strictly platonic. I was a little devastated but didn't want to give up having this unique person in my life just because she wasn't going to be my soul mate. She truly is my best friend.

Nowadays when I meet someone who excites me I try to step back and not jump in with both feet and an open heart. I make sure my romantic hopes don't overtake my rational thinking. If I'd really looked at who Cindy was as a person and who she wasn't I would have known we'd never make it as a couple.

It's been years since I've harbored romantic illusions about Cindy. But I will always hold a few regrets.

Cindy Says

I have a "male" attitude about dating. I've never needed a husband to complete me. Maybe that's why I've always found it easy to meet guys. I have fun and move on. This probably sounds odd considering I spent my prime dating years as a Mormon.

Although I was raised in Utah my parents were Catholic. My

dad was a jerk. He became physically and emotionally abusive to me. When I was twelve, he and Mom divorced. To the shock and horror of my parents I decided to convert. Mormonism gave me good values—honesty, integrity, ethics, and the urge to help my fellow man. But Mormons have misogynist views toward women. I should know. I was engaged—boom, boom, boom!—to three Mormons before I was twenty-nine.

That's when I left the religion and started leading a normal life. I've devoted prime energy to building a successful career as a journalist. Men have been my diversion, not my avocation.

I was thirty-five when Dan became one of my diversions. A mutual friend thought Dan and I would hit it off, so she introduced us.

I liked him from the start. But I was dating other guys, including a TV news reporter. I told Joe, the reporter, that I was seeing his new boss. But Dan knew nothing about Joe and this created problems.

For example, one morning Dan popped over unexpectedly with a bag of bagels and said jauntily, "Let's go hiking." Joe had gone home just a few hours earlier and left his glasses on my coffee table. The frames had been treated to make them nonreflective for the TV cameras so they were very distinctive. Thankfully Dan didn't notice them but it was close.

Eventually Dan found out I was dating his employee. I was more into Joe on a romantic level but it would have been ludicrous for him to sacrifice his job for a woman he'd been dating two months. Not that Dan would have fired him, but it's not a great career move to schtup your boss' girlfriend. I told Joe to give me up.

Dan was reasonable. He knew I'd been dating other people, just not someone in his backyard. But it set a bad pattern. Subsequently I never felt the need to be faithful to him. Dan and I never had the defining talk where we both agreed to be exclusive.

To be honest, Dan was great company but it began feeling like a duty romance. I enjoyed his company but was in it partially to save Joe's butt. It was like, "Joe isn't an option anymore so why not continue seeing Dan?"

To be *brutally* honest the sexual chemistry wasn't there for me. Dan has great physical hygiene but for some weird reason there was something about his personal smell—some musky odor—that while not being offensive, turned me off. I tried to get past it because Dan is such a quality human being.

To my best recollection the relationship turned platonic three to four months after we met. I'd started dating a great new guy and made the mistake of telling one of Dan's friends all about this new conquest. She went running to Dan, who for the first time ever got *livid*.

He said, "That you have no compunction about letting me erroneously believe we're in a monogamous relationship shows you have issues to resolve about men. I think you need psychiatric help. If you don't have good health benefits I'll pay for your treatment."

This shows what kind of guy Dan is: In the midst of feeling angry and betrayed he was still out to help me. I took him up on his offer and saw a shrink for ten months. In therapy I learned that it's okay to let a guy get close and to depend on him for certain things. Not all men are like my dad.

There is one positive I got from my father: He treated me horribly but I've chosen not to let hatred toward him ruin my life. We have the choice to either be happy or be miserable. It's not brain surgery. I've chosen to be happy.

My friendship with Dan makes me very happy. I got ten times more out of our aborted romance than he did. Dan literally pushed me toward pursuing mental health and personal growth.

I say to any single woman out there: Grab this guy.

Sherry Says

A dating couple should not assume that their other half is on exactly the same romantic wavelength. Trouble looms when this presumption is based not on communication in the concrete world of words and touch, but in the psychic zone inhabited by Dionne Warwick and her ilk.

Dan felt himself falling in love with Cindy. He figured since Cindy spent most of her free time with him, that she felt the same way. Cindy, living in a bubble of self-absorption, took her time puncturing his illusions.

Where Dan Erred

There is such a thing as being too trusting and laid-back. Commitment or no commitment, Dan had a right to get upset with Cindy for keeping silent about her affair with Joe. Didn't his ears burn wondering at the nature of the pillow-talk conversations between his employee and his lover? Dan's easy acceptance of this small betrayal, as Cindy put it, "set a bad pattern", allowing her to cheat without fear of serious repercussions.

Dan wasn't very good at reading romantic STOP signs from Cindy until they reached the equivalent of a verbal 2×4 with her literally screaming out her disinterest in moving in with him.

Sometimes you've got to ask the questions even if you're afraid you won't like the answers.

Where Dan Shone

This is a nice guy, yet not a patsy. He had his breaking point. Once Cindy exhibited what he deemed "crappy" behavior, he was outta there in the romantic sense but still caring enough about his ex to worry about her psychological well-being. Alas, I can't help wondering if his acceptance of the flawed nature of human beings would have extended to Joe had the latter not bailed on the romantic triangle.

Overall, Dan is kind, honest, dependable, spontaneous, giving, and forgiving. Hopefully his eventual next marriage will prove the third time to be lucky.

Where Cindy Erred

We are the products of our upbringing. Cindy's "male" (callous) dating attitude is the result of self-protection. Her male role models were an abusive father topped off by a trio of Mormon, misogynist ex-fiancés. Until she began dating Dan, she hadn't gone in much for self-examination of her relationship mores. Men were like a smorgasbord—she took what she craved, devoured it (sometimes swallowing the item whole), than moved on to the next dish.

Before getting horizontal with Dan, Cindy should have mentioned she was dating his employee. While I commend Cindy for not wanting Joe to lose his job, I can't applaud her for continuing a sexual liaison with Dan primarily to help Joe out of a career jam. On the surface such a move sounds sacrificial—and extremely ill advised. Sex for a third party's sake is pretty dysfunctional. To this "man-izer," what was one more lover?

Then and there, decency demanded she diplomatically end the romantic nature of her relationship with Dan. Barring that, she shouldn't have continued seeing him almost every night of the week, acting like a girlfriend while secretly dating the town. When news of this betrayal broke she exhibited scant regard for Dan's feelings.

The person who is less into the relationship should always ask herself if she's being diplomatic yet honest with the other person.

Thou Shalt Not Lead a Lover On may not make the top ten commandments, but the Higher Power would doubtless regard it as an indisputable relationship sin.

Where Cindy Shone

She was good company, always up for adventure. Cindy didn't want to hurt Dan by admitting he wasn't her sexual cup of tea. Although perhaps she could have diplomatically suggested he switch to a different deodorant.

Your Love Lesson From This Couple's Breakup

This is another instance of a former couple having vastly different recollections about the turning points in their relationship.

In one corner we have Cindy—who was so detached that she didn't even remember the length of her liaison with Dan. To Cindy, the triangle debacle with Joe was the beginning of the end. In Dan's mind, the "three's not company" interlude was a speed bump on the road to what he assumed would become lasting love. He saw the house-hunting incident as the nail being put in the wall, and the day Cindy left him with cold pizza and a broken heart as the nail being hammered home. Until prodded, Cindy didn't even remember either of those events.

If Cindy and Dan had checked in with each other about their varying takes on the relationship, Dan would have likely spared himself pain by checking out on the relationship much, much sooner.

Chapter 12

If None of Your Friends Can Stand Your Latest, There's Probably a Reason

Cindy Says

During the four years between my relationships with Dan and Tim I dated countless men, sleeping with approximately 30 percent of them. When I turned forty it seemed time to get serious. I'd dated *everybody* in town. So in the course of researching an article on Internet dating I placed an on-line personal.

On paper Tim was *perfect*—a former model currently working in the film industry. And he was a wonderfully romantic cyber-lover, sending passionate sonnets and photos of couples kissing under waterfalls. I had such high hopes.

We seemed to have so much in common. Tim was a lapsed Mormon. He was also funny, bright, and creative—traits I love. Our E-mails and phone calls got increasingly erotic.

Two months after the first contact Tim flew out to stay with me.

We spent the weekend in bed having sex. I should have paid attention to the fact that he had family in town but made no attempt to contact them.

Every other weekend either Tim or I would get on a plane. One day he said, "You're not going anywhere career-wise in Utah. Why not come live with me? We'll be insanely happy and make love morning, noon, and night. And I'll get you a job in film."

I thought, *Why the heck not? I've never lived with anyone. If not with Tim, then who?* Plus Utah was a dead end for me both personally and professionally. So I ignored the sage advice of my friends who kept saying, "Cindy, what do you really know about this guy?"

The second I moved in Tim became totally impotent. To get anything out of him required a three-hour handjob while he channel-surfed.

It became glaringly apparent that Tim wasn't up to snuff in many areas of life. He had neither friends nor social skills. He didn't even know enough to say "good morning" or "good night." He'd leave the house on Friday night without telling me. I'd ask later, "Aren't we a couple? Shouldn't we be doing things together on the weekend?" He'd bark, "No one keeps tabs on me."

Tim gave me a closet but not much else. I wasn't allowed to have any of my personal belongings around. I'd try to hang a painting and he'd say it didn't match his décor. His décor was ratty furniture and walls he half painted seven years ago.

He never finished anything—from decorating his apartment to grad school to moving forward on the Internet commerce site we were trying to put together. Even though I was new in town I was able to set up meetings for us with money people. Tim was hopeless at pitching his ideas. He couldn't even finish writing a business plan.

Although Tim had been honest about his life in broad strokes, when I looked to fill in the picture there were blank spots. Yes, he was in the film business. But not a line producer, as he said. My boyfriend was a gofer making an hourly wage.

Los Angeles is a town based on power and influence. Tim had neither. He worked ungodly hours but no one had respect for him. Eventually he got laid off.

The last straw came two months after I moved in with him. I had just written an article for a woman's magazine on how to seduce your man. I put on a sexy negligee and thought, *It's now or never.*

Tim pushed me away. He was in "monk mode."

I left the house and stayed with a friend all weekend. When I returned, I moved into the spare bedroom. Tim said that wasn't how he wanted things to be but maybe it was for the best. His exact words: "I think God is keeping me from sinning by preventing me from having sex with a woman I'm not married to."

It took me another four months before I bought my condo. During that period Tim would do passive-aggressive things like lock me in my room. If a date picked me up at the house Tim would freak out and insult the guy.

My new California friends would say things like, "This guy is severely depressed. He's not all there." Tim introduced me to his "best buddies." Privately these buddies said things to me like, "We hardly know the guy. He's weird. You're not really living with him, are you?"

My judgment is usually much better. But I was at a point of really wanting to share my life with someone. And the illusion, the man Tim seemed to be, was so good that I ignored all the evidence that he was kind of crazy.

I look on my relationship with Tim as an emotional fart, an aberration. Basically my life has been a full one. Good things happen to me. Enduring a few months of emotional hell was a small price to pay to get me where I should be in my life—Los Angeles.

Tim Says

I was raised traditionally—marriage or bust. So far it's been bust, which is fine. I've learned to accept the joys of relationships and their subsequent endings without allowing it to impact the rest of my life.

I'm forty-seven and have had a goodly number of relationships. At approximately the six-month mark, when the lust settles so to speak, emotional gravity takes over and women are forced to show you who they really are. At that point things rapidly deteriorate.

Once or twice I felt strongly enough about someone to contemplate marriage. That's when she wriggled out of the straitjacket. Just kidding. I've never lived with someone—unless you count the period of time last year when Cindy shared my home.

Cindy and I met through mutual friends. I was on the Internet researching information on a Utah athlete who had died. Cindy's name came up because of her work as a journalist. We began E-mailing and eventually spoke on the phone. A few months into this long-distance interface I had to visit her town on business. It seemed an opportune moment to finally look Cindy in the eyes.

At first sight I was struck by her intelligence and wit. She has a wonderful command of the language. We spoke about restaurants, Southern California, film, politics. It's hard to recall but during my brief sojourn in Utah I might have moved out of my hotel into Cindy's apartment.

In subsequent months it's possible I returned once or twice to Utah . . . and Cindy might have ventured to California to gather information for an article. Primarily, though, we communicated by phone and E-mail until Cindy decided that California held better career opportunities for her than Utah.

Because it's difficult to find an affordable place in the L.A. area I invited Cindy to stay with me. It was clear this was more a matter of real estate than romance. We were lovers, true, but there was never any sort of treaty of alliance outlining the specifics of exclusivity between us. Although when you are dating one person and don't care less about meeting anyone else cohabiting can be a natural occurrence.

I value my privacy a great deal but the adjustment to cohabiting was easier for me than Cindy. She commented several times that she missed having her stuff close by. My place didn't feel like home to her. I said that was unfortunate but also the way things were. I didn't have room to hang her various knickknacks. The subject of looking for a place together to accommodate all our belongings never arose.

Cindy couldn't adapt to the world I've created. For instance I got slammed for giving her too much rope. According to her I wasn't proprietary enough. I didn't get jealous when she'd go out with guy friends. Yet if I'd have said, "No, stay here with me," I would have been labeled *controlling*.

I believe in the concept of a fairy-tale romance where the couple naturally adapts to each other's rhythms. If you have to force something to work, it's not working.

I'm fairly certain the suggestion that Cindy move out of my bed into my spare bedroom came from me. It was a follow-up to the reality of the situation. Cindy was very tense—the result of being uprooted in both her literal residence and career path. Her being so on-edge made me nervous.

I can't recall how long it took Cindy to move from my spare bedroom to her condo—a month, a year? Boy, am I forgetting time. In my defense, I was constantly working. I'm what is called a line producer and when a film or TV series is in production, I'm out the door at 5 A.M. and not home until midnight. It's all-consuming. Before you know it, not just a year is gone but a decade.

Why do relationships end? The reason could be something as seemingly trivial as a fickleness in attitude. I've dated women who treated our eventual breakup as offhandedly as a lunch date falling through. That sort of person is not someone you can depend on.

Cindy is overflowing with great qualities. She is a great catch, but ultimately someone I found it necessary to cast back into the sea.

Sherry Says

When a person has the desire to be swept off her feet, the next guy she meets will likely be drafted as official feet-sweeper, regardless of his qualifications for the job. Cindy had self-sprinkled fairy dust in her eyes. Her romantic judgment was thus dangerously impaired and she saw only what (whom!) she wanted to see: Prince Charming.

That's why a gal's gotta not just have clear-sighted friends, she's gotta *listen* to them.

Punch/Counterpunch

TIM: I visited Utah on business and it was a nice opportunity to meet Cindy.

CINDY: The only reason he came out was to see me. He had it all set up, from what restaurants we should eat in and what positions we should have sex in.

CINDY: I would have remained in Utah if Tim hadn't repeatedly begged me to move in with him so that he could lavish me with great sex and fun times.

TIM: Before she came out to California, I was specific with Cindy that she should not relocate if the move would be solely because of me.

TIM: We had mutual friends in common.

CINDY: He has no friends.

CINDY: I E-mail him once a month.

TIM: Since Cindy left my apartment, we've become the closest of friends.

TIM: My parents' marriage was a role model of what a good relationship should be.

CINDY: He hates the way his dad treats his mom. He never sees his family. He spends Christmas all alone.

Where Cindy Erred

Having spent the bulk of her adult years as a commitment-phobe (see the previous chapter) it's not shocking that when Cindy hit the big 4-0 and decided it was time to enter a serious relationship, she chose a partner practically incapable of tying his own shoes. Personal growth generally proceeds at a one step forward, two steps back, two steps forward, one step back clip. Cindy learned the hard way that a precondition for a relationship between two people to bloom is that they *both* enjoy good mental health.

Before moving in with someone, it's wise to get to know him slowly, ferret out an accurate assessment of his flaws and strengths rather than to base a life decision on a handful of romantic weekends. Cindy, like Tim, saw in the other an idealized image of a lover, not the real person.

She ignored all warning signs that underneath his pretty packaging Tim was a gift that was no prize.

Where Cindy Shone

Happily, Cindy has never been the whiny, needy sort. Even more happily, therapy and life experience led to real growth on her part. She was much less egocentric in this relationship than in ones previous. She allowed herself to be vulnerable and truly attempted to be Tim's partner in ways that extended beyond the bedroom. She tried to make Tim's home *their* home, to share quality time as a couple, and to run a business with her man. When these endeavors didn't work, Cindy cut her losses. She got out quickly and relatively unscathed.

Her basic attitude that life is good and she is blessed is a good one to maintain. She now wants a man with whom to share her life, yet she won't fall apart without a partner. Anyone who is in a solid, nurturing relationship will get there because she or he was first happy as a single person.

Where Tim Erred

Tim and Cindy's version of the "facts" behind the relationship differ in many respects. To wit: Tim initially contended that he met Cindy through friends. No, wait, he met her while researching a story on-line about athletes. Obviously it's a hop, skip and, cyber-click from a news Web site to a matchmaking one.

This lie is understandable. It's a trifle embarrassing to admit you needed the personals to find love. However, that doesn't explain fib numbers two to infinity. For example, Tim gave Cindy the impression he was open to creating a loving, lustful relationship. There is evidence he uttered the phrase: "Live with me and we'll be insanely happy and make love morning, noon, and night."

He uses distant, stiff language to describe one of the most significant relationships in his life: "I've never lived with someone— unless you count the period of time last year when Cindy shared my home."

Straight talk is obviously not easy for him. Before asking his lover to wing across the country, he should have admitted he had hang-ups about living with a woman not his wife. He also should have admitted he was a gofer, not bragged that he was a high-powered movie executive who could get her a job. Additionally, it might have been wise for him to attempt acting like part of a couple versus leaving Cindy alone on the weekends, then barking when she protested, "No one keeps tabs on me."

Tim believes the words he speaks. He lives in Tim World—a place that resembles Los Angeles but is an alternate reality peopled by, guess whom? In Tim World contradictions abound: He doesn't allow breakups to emotionally impact the rest of his life, yet rails against women who treat the demise of a romance as offhandedly as a lunch date falling through. He is looking for a fairy-tale love that requires no work to maintain. Alas, love like that occurs only in fairy-tales.

Where Tim Shone

He opened up his home if not his heart to Cindy. It is an issue of trust to allow someone to physically "invade" your premises. And when things didn't click between the couple he allowed Cindy to stay for months and months in his spare bedroom (okay, he lost track of time) before she found her own place.

Your Love Lesson From This Couple's Breakup

In trustworthy friends you should trust. They have your best interests at heart.

Before Cindy left Utah, her best buds asked a reasonable question, "What do you know about this guy?" She didn't answer that question—to them or, more importantly, to herself.

After uprooting her body and belongings to California, new acquaintances also warned her off Tim. She chose not to listen. It's pure dumb luck that Cindy emerged relatively unscathed from a relationship she'd never have entered if she'd listened to sense-spouting chums.

My Biggest Heartbreak and What It Taught Me About Love

Shawn Stinson, 36, tourism industry executive

The entire time my ex-wife and I were courting, we lived in different states. So, until our wedding in 1991 each time we got together was like a vacation. Our expectations of what marriage would be like were miles apart. I work in the tourism industry—it involves long hours, lots of socializing, and lots of travel. Debbie is a schoolteacher who likes one key friend in her life—preferably a husband. There's nothing wrong with that but we had basic incompatibilities. Three months after the wedding we should have still been on our honeymoon. Instead we were constantly fighting. We tried a marriage counselor but . . .

Debbie and I spent six years together but she now regards me as the devil incarnate. I'm the cheating, lying bastard who disrupted her life, yanked her from California to Utah, then initiated a divorce. If she needs me to be the bad guy, that's fine.

Couples can work through certain things like which brand of toothpaste to use. But if two people have core issues that divide them—intimacy, job, sexual—those are much harder to resolve. If Debbie and I had laid our cards on the table; heck, at least lived in the same state, we probably would have realized that marriage between us probably wasn't a bright idea.

Peter & Karen
Relationship b: 1996; d: 1999

Chapter 13

You Can't Get Blood from a Stone

Peter Says

Before Karen, I never dated anyone for more than a year—and usually for just a few months. Basically, I'm fairly independent: Seinfeld, pre–Jessica Sklar—your basic bachelor. Marriage and the house in the suburbs scenario never held any attraction for me. I value my freedom. But I'm not the type to string a woman along. Everyone I ever dated knew where I was coming from—including Karen.

People who have been single their whole life have a tendency to be self-centered, as there's no one else they have to please. As for sex . . . When you're single, it's feast or famine. When you're married, you get it all the time. I guess that's why Karen took me home with her the night we met. I was the first guy she met after her divorce so I became her rebound lover.

What's great about Karen is that she loves to do things. We

traveled all around the country and when we were in New York there were always movies, the theater, and parties. Karen gets invited to lots of parties, and having been married all those years, she was used to showing up with a man on her arm.

What's not so great about Karen is that she always wanted more than I could give. She needs someone by her side 24/7. Psychologically I think that need stems from her childhood. Her mom was pretty old, forty, when Karen was born. Karen's dad died when she was very young, and by the time she was a teenager, her two older brothers were out of the house. So she grew up in turmoil, with a tendency to analyze everything and desperate for company. Which is why she got married at twenty.

I had a normal upbringing. My family was always around and my dad died just a few years ago. Nothing out of the ordinary happened so I never developed deep psychological issues. I'm a simple guy with simple needs.

One major thing Karen doesn't grasp is that, coming from a different background and life history, my mind-set is not the same as hers. She doesn't *get* that you can't tell someone who's thirty-eight, thirty-nine, forty, and set in his ways, "I'm looking for a soul mate, a man who's on my wavelength. I want you to become introspective. I want you to be with me all the time and tell me certain things I need to hear. . . ."

When I didn't do what was asked, she'd become very emotional. Karen doesn't accept the word *no* very easily. This aggressive tendency serves her well in business but on a personal level . . . let's just say she's not very forgiving of people's attitudes when they diverge from hers.

At first it was difficult spending nearly every night with Karen. I felt like I was on a leash. Eventually it didn't feel like a choke collar. I learned it could be nice having someone there all the time. It was a lot of fun hanging out with Karen. But I never stopped being a person who has an independent streak. And she never stopped seeing my need for space as a rejection of her.

I want it on record that I was faithful to Karen the entire time we were together. I'm not promiscuous. I've always been a classic serial monogamist. I know Karen found it suspicious that we always hung out at her place. But keeping her away from my apartment wasn't a privacy issue. I didn't have another woman stashed in the closet. But the place was always a mess.

Our basic problem was that Karen defined a relationship as leading to marriage and I defined it as dating more seriously but not necessarily leading to marriage. After six months Karen was dropping hints about the M word, and referring to my mom as her future mother-in-law. I didn't see her mom as *my* future in-law. So it was sad but probably inevitable that we'd break up. But I could have kept going the way we were indefinitely.

The thing that really steamed Karen was when I planned a solo five-week vacation to Saudi Arabia without consulting her. Why didn't I say anything? Right before I was due to leave, Karen and I were going to Wyoming together. I didn't want the whole weekend to be marred by her tears and constant badgering for me either not to go or to go for less time. I didn't want to listen to three days of, "You'd rather go away alone than be with me." I wasn't rejecting her; solo trips are just something I do. But I knew she'd see it as either/or. In my mind I didn't lie to her; I was just trying to crystallize everything in my head.

I am not a weirdo. There is nothing unique about a man who can't commit to marriage.

Did I love Karen? It's a funny thing. When you're twenty, love is hormonal. Your heart is driven by lust. When you age . . . A woman I know is in her sixties and told me she hasn't needed sex or love for a long time. Did I love Karen? I think so but I didn't feel, *Oh, my God, I must spend the next thirty years with her*. Yet, I miss not being with her every night.

To be honest, I didn't totally let Karen into my heart or soul. I needed inner space. Karen's never gone more than two minutes without being with a man. She's following the same pattern with her new boyfriend. Instead of letting things evolve, they're together every night. But from the little I know about him, I don't think this guy's going to wind up marrying her, either. Though Karen and I aren't speaking right now, if she came to me and wanted to pick up where we left off, I'd probably say yes.

If we did start over, I think I'd do everything pretty much the same way. Okay, maybe I'd shorten my vacations away from her. And maybe I wouldn't always be so stubborn when she asked me to do something like help move her mother into a new home.

Now that Karen's left me, I am questioning a few things. I am coming to understand that being with one person for a lifetime can be an okay thing. Most of my married friends are happy with their wives.

But the bottom line is that some confirmed bachelors, after breaking up with a woman over a refusal to commit, get an inner click that finally makes them pop that question of questions. After Karen and I split, I waited for that click. I'm still waiting.

Karen Says

I met Peter two months and two days after the breakup of an eighteen-year marriage to my childhood sweetheart. I was at an event to hear an author whose book I had edited read from his latest novel. Peter sat next to me. I noticed him right away but I also noticed a woman on his other side who I assumed was his date. Still, right before my author began his talk, I asked to borrow Peter's copy of *The New York Times Book Review*. After the lecture I returned the paper to Peter and he asked me out for coffee. I was obviously wrong about the woman. Making wrong calculations about things concerning Peter became a pattern for me.

Over coffee he and I talked about things that we'd never again discuss in our three years together—like about how people often say one thing and mean another.

That first night Peter came over to my place and essentially didn't leave for three years. Despite the hundreds of nights he stayed over, I was at his apartment a grand total of three times. He never let me have a key. And all he ever kept at my place was a toothbrush.

We came from different worlds. Peter, who's a podiatrist, was thirty-eight—my age—when we met, yet he'd never been in a serious relationship. I was also the first girlfriend in his life who'd ever been married. I'd catch him looking at me like I was this alien creature, a specimen labeled "Divorced Woman."

The early stages of our relationship were wonderful. The first month, we didn't leave my apartment. Afterward, he and I discovered a mutual love of travel. We drove all over the country, exploring funky, small towns. For New Year's one time we went to Charleston, North Carolina. Peter planned and paid for everything. He was always generous in a monetary sense.

But he never introduced me to his friends, never insisted his widowed mother include me in their holiday get-togethers, was hardly ever there when I *really* needed him. Like, when my mother developed Alzheimer's, he flew to California a few times with me to visit her. But it was clearly under duress. And when I moved her to New York I had to ask a different friend to help me get my mom settled.

As long as Peter and I didn't define what we had together as a "relationship," things were great. He said, and kept repeating, "I'm never going to be your boyfriend. What we have will always just be dating." I guess "dating" includes spending nearly every night together for three years.

I spent a lot of those years crying. Most people in my life think of me as this happy, fun person. Peter thought of me as a depressed,

weeping person. With him I was. He never told me I was beautiful. He never made me feel smart or truly loved or wanted. My
husband had been a very doting, affectionate person, so this was
tough to handle.

It often felt like I was taming a wild horse. Each small step I'd
get him to take toward intimacy—to put his arm around my
shoulders in the movie theater, come over if I was sick, fall asleep
holding me instead of staying on the other side of the bed—happened only after lots of pushing on my part and backing away on
his. Eventually Peter would realize he enjoyed these things, too.
All on his own, he started rubbing the back of my head while we
were driving. But it was all such an effort. I longed for someone
who could give love naturally, not just respond to learned cues.

His making changes did give me hope. I clung to the belief that
one day Peter would stop guarding his singleness like some pre-
cious gem and we'd get married. I wanted to believe that because
I did love him and we had so many areas of compatibility. But
there were also so many areas where I could make no headway.
Peter's a very private person who doesn't like to share what he's
thinking. He's also evasive. I'd listen to him on the phone lying to
his mother about why he'd be late getting to her house and I'd
wonder what he lied to *me* about. Ultimately he lied to me about
something *huge*.

I don't want this to come out wrong. Peter is a good person.
But he's very disconnected from his feelings and from what he
truly wants and what would truly make him happy. Too many
times he'd do something hurtful, I'd cry, and he'd apologize and
promise to try harder. Inevitably he'd break the promise.

Ironically, the last straw came about because of the thing we
loved most—travel. Every fall Peter takes an exotic, five-week
long trip—Lebanon, Bosnia . . . The first year we were together I
obviously had no claim on him, so he took off and didn't send
even one postcard. The second year I begged him to shorten his

trip to three weeks and spend the rest of the time with me. My tears wet his shirt but didn't dampen his travel plans. The third year his usual departure time was just two weeks away and he hadn't mentioned the trip. I was thrilled. I assumed this meant he'd spend his vacation time with me.

At the last moment he dropped the bomb: He was leaving in three days for Saudi Arabia. It was a fait accompli. It was too late for me to get him to change his plans. I felt lied to and totally unloved. He barely noticed that I broke up with him. He was too preoccupied with last-minute details for the great excursion.

I thought if there was any chance to salvage the relationship, Peter would at least keep in touch from Saudi Arabia. I'd asked him to call while he was away. I was worried because it's a dangerous area. I received no postcard, no phone call. When Peter came back he kept going on and on about what a great trip it had been. It barely resonated for him that we were over. By that point I'd met Tim, my current boyfriend.

Four months later Peter doesn't realize he ended our relationship by disconnecting from me. How else can you explain his lying to me about the trip? He insists I'm the one who wanted out; his desire was to go on as we were. There is now a lot of ill feeling between us, which I hope will eventually fade.

I believe Peter is truly suffering; he misses what we had. He misses me so much that if I came back he'd finally be able to turn off the switch in his head that keeps him from being capable of love. I believe he'd marry me and that I would make him happy. But I'd be crazy to become his wife. He didn't appreciate me enough when we were together before, so why would that change?

If I had those three years to do over, I wouldn't have spent them trying so hard to get Peter to change his personality. You can't get blood from a stone. I also wouldn't have cried so much.

I got a lot from the relationship—it helped me heal from my

divorce, and I learned I could be in a relationship with someone who didn't dote on me. My new boyfriend, Tim, is a doter. He's constantly complimenting me and touching me and making me feel special. Just yesterday he sent me an E-greeting that said, "You are the light of my life." It was simple to do, and cost nothing, yet the gesture meant the world to me.

I taught Peter a lot about himself. By the end of our relationship I knew him better than he knew himself. Again, he'd be much happier if he were married to me. I know I made a difference in his life—I hope it's a positive one.

I believe that 90 percent of what we call love is both partners making a commitment to each other; to being part of a team. If only Peter had been willing to be my teammate . . .

Punch/Counterpunch

KAREN: His battle cry of not being the marrying kind gives him license to live in an irresponsible manner. He's afraid to look into himself and admit what would make him happy, which is me.

PETER: She can't accept that I didn't love her enough to want to marry her.

PETER: Everything was about how it reflected on her, not about my perhaps equally valid point of view. Sometimes a guy's just gotta spend time alone.

KAREN: He knows he's the one who missed out.

Sherry Says

Karen and Peter are two people functioning well within the range of normal neurotic behavior. Even more promising, these are two people that genuinely cared about each other and genuinely enjoyed spending time together—at least when they were on vacation.

That would be enough if a relationship were one big road trip. But, as the many couples who've tried and failed at love can attest, as well as those who've tried and succeeded, a relationship is so much more. A relationship can work (notice the word *work*) if the couple possess an ability to empathize with each other's point of view and, of course, share common relationship objectives.

Where Peter Erred

This hapless lug thought he was on a three-year-long first date. It is hard for him to realize that you do owe the person with whom you are living more than a weekend in Wyoming. You owe her courtesy, respect, and *honesty*. You truly invite the person who shares your bed into your life (introduce her to your friends, for pity's sake!). And you do take her feelings into consideration before booking a solo flight for five weeks. Or you will, as Peter did, find yourself permanently flying solo.

Where Peter Shone

He knows his own psyche. He's a simple guy with simple life goals that don't include marriage. And he never made false promises to Karen about the nature of his intentions toward her.

Where Karen Erred

She is, as Peter pointed out, a woman who's "never gone more than two minutes without a man." Since she so rashly jumped into a relationship before the marital bedsheets were even stripped, it is providential that she didn't make a poorer choice for companion than Peter. Since I haven't interviewed Tim, I can't render an informed opinion on the potential durability of her latest liaison, although I can express the wish that she'd allow herself time to live as Karen, single person, before morphing into Karen, half of couple. If she grew comfortable and confident on her own before looking for love, she'd be more clear-sighted about the type of man with whom she could build a happy future.

Karen aptly points out that Peter has trouble defining "relationship" but she has equal difficulty understanding "dating." If she had slowly gotten to know Peter, his hopes, goals, habits, etc., before inviting him and his toothbrush over to live, it would have been easier to accept much earlier on that he couldn't give her the things she craved most from a lover. (For instance the ability to commit not just body but soul.) Instead, emotionally hooked on this inappropriate man from night one, she was powerless to cut bait and run. This "love-blindness" caused her to never see Peter clearly, and rendered her incapable of appreciating the many good qualities he undoubtedly possesses. The only ones she mentions are his love of travel and financial generosity.

Karen is a walking advertisement for the futility of trying to transform the nature of another human being. As the joke goes, a lightbulb has to *want* to change. And the conceit she displays by claiming to know better than Peter what would make him happy—well, good luck, Tim.

Where Karen Shone

Karen is capable of unashamedly giving and receiving copious amounts of affection and love. And she is unafraid to speak her mind and to ask for what she needs. Plus, she is capable of growth. Peter's ex-girlfriend now understands that if both partners can't (won't) make a commitment to being part of a team, one of them is going to eventually stage a mutiny.

Your Love Lesson From This Couple's Breakup

The healthiest couples love each other, flaws and all. If their goals don't mesh, they accept that and move on, versus frantically trying to change the other person "for his or her own good."

Chapter 14

To Forgive Too Readily Is Not Always Divine

Sheila Says

I tend to get involved with men who are in some kind of trouble and Dave was no exception. The way we met was somewhat strange. I was living off campus with my college boyfriend Josh. Dave was our landlord. Josh was out a lot, working on the school paper so Dave and I hung out together most evenings. Nothing romantic happened at that time, but I definitely felt a passionate pull toward him.

After graduation I moved to New York to launch a career in publishing. Josh stayed behind to get his MBA. A few months later Dave moved to New York and looked me up. He wanted to pen the Great American Novel. I pumped up his confidence about his writing skills and helped him find a job at the trade magazine where I worked as an editor.

Dave often complained about the state of his love life—women rarely wanted to date him. For some reason this drew me to him more and more. I broke up with my long-distance boyfriend and started seeing Dave. After six months I felt we were ready for the next step. I broached us moving in together, not as an ultimatum, but as a subject for discussion.

He got totally crazy, shrieking that he wasn't sure he could handle monogamy or commitment. To prove his point while he was on a business trip, he slept with a prostitute, then confessed the lurid details to me.

This *should* have been a clue that he wasn't relationship material. Instead of giving Dave the boot I analyzed the reasons for his indiscretion. I decided he was putting the brakes on our relationship out of fear; his emotions were driving him to get in too deep. In other words, he had slept with the hooker not because he didn't care about me but because he cared too much.

I forgave him. We continued dating exclusively and Dave continued saying he'd always be the cheating kind. I believed, and still do that Dave essentially has a monogamous nature. During a short trip out of town to visit friends. Dave called and said, "When you get back let's move in together."

I had a great apartment and Dave lived in a dive, so he moved into my place. A major problem for me was his extreme slovenliness. Another huge hurdle: Dave had spent a lot of time by himself and consequently developed rituals, which he'd cling to as a way of avoiding loneliness. He had a *very* regimented schedule and no tolerance for anything that interfered with his routine. Like at a certain time of day he *had* to drink a martini. At parties he'd be obnoxiously opinionated, not caring if he offended people. I still cringe remembering his ribald rant about an old Indian chief and penises, given in front of a woman he'd never met before. She was so bothered by his diatribe that she put her hands over her ears. If I tried to correct his behavior he'd become furious.

The first year was hell with lots of fighting. Dave frequently threatened to leave. After the third or fourth threat I said, "Go." Eventually things settled down and we learned each other's limits. He didn't become Felix Unger, but he did stop leaving the dishes from dinner on the table until the following morning.

For the next few years things were fairly smooth. Dave has a tender, homey streak he doesn't show until he's known someone a while. He's a great cook and would make a feast every Sunday night for our friends and family. And we'd go antique shopping in the country on weekends.

However, somewhere around year four of living together I began to feel dissatisfied. We were both writers and extremely competitive with each other. A truly vicious streak came out when we played racquetball. We got so angry we had to stop the game. More distressingly, I wanted to talk about feelings and where our relationship was going and whether we would ever marry and have a child. At one point he said I could lie and tell people we were married. I said I'd rather *be* married and pretend we weren't.

The wife and kids bit didn't appeal to Dave's image of himself as a rake. An editor who expressed interest in publishing Dave's novel asked him to write a dedication. Dave wrote down everyone in his life except me! I was kind of insulted.

Our sex life began going south around this time. I had a pregnancy scare. I hoped I was; Dave hoped I wasn't. That brought home the crucial issue for me: I wanted children and Dave didn't.

Around this time a friend told me that Dave had made a pass at her. She begged me not to tell him I knew, so I was silently furious. But I confessed an infidelity I'd committed with an ex around the time Dave slept with the hooker. Dave didn't let on that this bothered him, but right after that I found out that two years earlier Dave had slept with a woman he'd met through me! She wasn't a close friend, but she knew all my intimates so the sting of betrayal was very sharp.

We argued a lot about my weight. I'm heavy and kept telling Dave he had to love me the way I was. His response was that he didn't find me sexy.

Dave finally agreed to try couples therapy. I cried through the whole first session because I realized how much easier it was to talk to the shrink than to my boyfriend. It was immediately, painfully obvious that the main thing keeping us together was inertia. Because we got along on a lot of levels, it seemed easier not to rock the boat. Yet therapy made it clear that we'd stayed together by not asking the hard questions, and by tabling the bedrock divisive issues of marriage and children.

Because of what we uncovered in therapy we acknowledged our relationship was over but lived together for another month while Dave looked for an apartment. I'd wanted to sleep together one last time during this period but it never happened. Dave chose to immediately go back to the way it was before we became romantically involved: him complaining about how hard it was to meet women, and me listening sympathetically, which wasn't comfortable for me. My friends were relieved when Dave finally moved out. They considered him an abrasive, difficult person.

Since our split, I believe Dave has deteriorated. He's become even more intense and eccentric, palling around with people from The Church of Satan. He's also drinking more. We broke up years ago and Dave has yet to be in a serious relationship. I'm about to marry my boyfriend of the past four years. Dave is very jealous of this relationship.

Looking back, I realize I twisted myself into knots trying to make things work. There has to be a dividing line between making a compromise and compromising yourself to a warped degree.

I forgave Dave for sleeping with the hooker and for so many other things out of a lack of self-confidence and because I loved him. I didn't want to be partnerless and so I took a partner who was bad for and to me.

Dave Says

I thought being with Sheila would be good, the way taking a dose of nasty medicine is good for you. And my assumption was correct—the relationship was an unpleasant experience from which I benefited. Our five years together taught me to be a more responsible person. I learned a bit about how to get along with people. That's an ongoing process. By the time you figure it all out, you're dead.

I'd never had a serious relationship before I met Sheila; just occasional liaisons. When we met, she was engaged to this fellow whom she really didn't want to end up marrying. I typically go for slender, Nordic types; Sheila is dark and full-figured. *Very* full-figured.

My theory is that we found each other convenient. When you're starving, you'll lunge for the first crumbs at hand. The tide didn't change; I never really found Sheila attractive. But she was interesting and easy to be with so I figured, why not?

Barely before we'd begun dating, Sheila was using strong-arm tactics to press for a commitment. She dragged me to her shrink, hoping that would convince me I was nuts if I didn't decide to live with her. Still, we'd gotten to the point where we'd agreed to keep our separate places. Then I got cold feet thinking how grim it would be without a girlfriend, how most of the women out there are losers, and I could do worse than Sheila. And most importantly, compared to my crummy apartment, Sheila lived in a palace. She was willing to let me share her digs for a minimal financial contribution.

I don't recall asking Sheila's forgiveness after I slept with the hooker. It was no big deal. I confessed out of a faint hope she would then be disabused of the notion of living with me.

Despite what she thinks, I wasn't afraid of commitment; just of commitment to *her*. Maybe for a short time I loved or lusted for her. But emotions didn't enter into our arrangement. She was a fairly stable person, well off, and I had no one else.

Sheila knew my routines well before we moved in together. Sometimes I would try to cooperate with her behavioral demands. Sometimes I wouldn't, hoping that would make her throw me out. Contrary to what she says, I didn't threaten to leave all that often . . . and she certainly never opened the door and said, "Go!"

I have some good memories. When we weren't fighting we could have fun together. I'd cook for her, give her massages, and occasionally buy her a cheap piece of jewelry. And we were intellectually compatible. But I knew that eventually Sheila and I would break up. She wanted marriage and kids and becoming a father was as appealing to me as contracting cancer. Kids yell, cry, break things, and are a horrible financial burden. And pregnancy makes women look fat. As for marriage—well, my parents stayed together thirty-nine years but they never looked happy. My mother, who was a depressive, gloried in her unhappiness.

To my mind, Sheila gloried in holding on to grudges. Men forgive and forget. Women keep the mental shit around and throw it like stink bombs at every opportunity. I'm not saying I'm perfect but I would fight about the matter at hand, not an incident from four years earlier. Sheila was the dirtiest fighter I'd ever seen. And she liked to fight—I'd tiptoe through each day in a vain effort not to have a major conflagration.

She's extremely giving—but will demand the shirt off your back in return for her "generosity." Sheila needs a lot of attention. She's one of those people who beats you over the head with a stick while yelling, "Love me, love me!"

The one area where Sheila and I found an easy compatibility was work. We're both writers but there was no competitiveness. We were careful not to compete for each other's clients. Occasionally, we still throw each other leads.

Neither of us was entirely monogamous during the relationship. I didn't give a crap who she slept with. By the time we moved in together the little desire I felt for her had faded. It got to the point I had to force myself to have sex with her.

She'd complain we didn't have sex often enough to suit her. I'd tell her it was in large part because she was fat. Sheila would then berate me for destroying her self-esteem. In reckless disregard to my needs, she got involved in some fat acceptance group—going whole hog, so to speak.

Sheila and I could have had a wonderful relationship if only we'd loved each other. That was the missing ingredient. And because we didn't love each other I resented that I was living with her. I felt stuck, angry with myself for being dragged kicking and screaming into this situation, and angry with her for not letting me go.

I agreed to couples counseling because I owed her that much. During the first session we both just said, "Oh, fuck it," at the same time.

Splitting up wasn't the least bit traumatic for me. I moved out twelve days afterward. I was so relieved that I'd never have to fight about not wanting to have sex with her again. All we were cut out to be was friends. I'm not the least bit jealous of her fiancé, although I have to admit my love life sucks. If I had a dollar for every woman who has said I'm the nicest guy in the world but they don't want to sleep with me, I'd be rich. The truth: They'd rather have a gaping wound in their chest than sleep with me. I'm not bad looking. It's something about my personality that makes me unattractive. I'm dating a woman now. She is the first one I've ever asked to marry me. So far she keeps saying no.

Living with Sheila enabled me to leave an apartment that could best be described as a place of squalor. I happily embraced the yuppie lifestyle.

I didn't give Sheila as much attention and affection as she

wanted. She deserved that from the person she lived with but I couldn't do it because I didn't love her. Even if it means always being alone I will never again get deeply involved with someone I don't love.

Punch/Counterpunch

SHEILA: Since our breakup, he's gotten more eccentric and angry.
DAVE: She spends too much time analyzing me, and not enough time trying to figure out her own flaws.

DAVE: I slept with the hooker because I wanted sex with an attractive woman. It was no big deal.
SHEILA: I drove him to sleep with the hooker to get back at me for pressuring him to move in together. It wasn't an act of betrayal but of hostility toward me.

Sherry Says

This couple was done in by their dueling mantras: "I don't love me." "No, I don't love me more." Sheila's self-esteem was so low it drove her to not just tolerate, but embrace abusive behavior in her partner, while Dave's abysmal self-image caused him to chase away the only person willing to dig for the good stuff (supposedly) hidden beneath his chalk-against-a-blackboard personality.

As anyone familiar with the dismal Manhattan housing situation knows, of the two people locked into this arid alliance outwardly Dave got the better deal: A great apartment practically rent-free. Sheila received something less tangible but infinitely more valuable in the long term: The knowledge of how low she would sink, how much she would swallow, forgive, so as not to be "partnerless." Memo to Sheila: It's better to be alone than saddled with a sadistic, selfish partner.

Where Sheila Erred

When you ask a man to move in to your abode and his response is to sleep with a hooker, that's not just a warning light, but a bona fide sign from God flashing in gaudily lit, king-sized letters: "DON'T DO IT!" Yet instead of racing from the danger, Sheila dashed pell-mell into certain doom.

Her fear of being alone overruled her self-dignity, sense of self-preservation—pretty much anything beginning with "self." She allowed her analytical abilities to obfuscate common sense: *He had slept with the hooker not because he didn't care about me but because he cared too much.* The pathetic ballsiness of this self-deceiving proclamation summons me to use the word *balderdash*.

Sheila candidly and graphically discusses the ways Dave hurt her. We hear about his cruel, crude nature, quirky regimens, and continual large and small snubbings of his live-in love (i.e.; not including Sheila in his book dedication). Then there was his utter disinterest in marriage and children—the things that mattered most to her. Sheila says she loved him but never offers up *why* other than that after a few years together she was able to penetrate his prickly disposition and discover his homey, tender side.

When Dave would open up and in his crude way tell her what he wanted (not to live together; for her to lose weight so he'd find her more attractive), she completely ignored the veracity of his desires to concentrate on how yet again he was wronging her.

Yet when Dave would do something untenable (i.e., make a pass at her friend), rather than reevaluate the depths of self-degradation she was willing to endure to keep the relationship going, she retaliated in a way meant to even the score. *I confessed an infidelity I'd committed with an ex around the time Dave slept with the hooker.*

It doesn't get much sadder or less healthy than that.

Where Sheila Shone

She had the patience to attempt to suss out whether or not the uncouth Dave was a diamond in the rough. Although he turned out not to be the hoped for jewel, award the lady some kudos for trying.

Another plus: Sheila wasn't wedded to the traditional male/female roles. She was fine with mentoring Dave careerwise, moving him into her apartment, and letting him cook her lavish meals.

Lastly, though saddled with cripplingly low self-esteem she didn't just lie back and take Dave's abuse but fought back. Unfortunately, not always in the wisest manner.

Where Dave Erred

If you don't love someone, don't allow yourself to be persuaded to move in together. If you do move in with her, treat the lady with some semblance of kindness, humanity, and respect. *She'd complain we didn't have sex often enough to suit her. I'd tell her it was in large part because she was fat.*

Dave doesn't think well of women, but he doesn't think well of himself, either. He's so armored against the slings and arrows he expects the world to hurl at him that he comes out slinging himself. It's almost impossible for him to display vulnerability, even (especially?) toward his life partner. Without displaying vulnerability, it's impossible to create a truly nurturing relationship.

Where Dave Shone

He never pretended to be someone he was not. Lord knows Dave lacks tact. Still, he was honest with Sheila about his limitations and needs.

Dave is someone, who though he strives mightily to make

himself as unlovable as he believes himself to be, has the courage of his own convictions—and is defiantly unapologetic about who he is.

Your Love Lesson From This Couple's Breakup

Listening to Sheila and Dave's versions of their relationship bears a resemblance to taking testimony from eyewitnesses to a car wreck: Each offers radically different interpretations of what they saw and experienced. Sheila: *We were both writers and extremely competitive with each other.* Dave: *The one area where we found easy compatibility was work.* There is even a dispute about how long they shared the same address after agreeing to break up.

One thing about which there is no dispute: If someone does something unforgivable to you (e.g., sleeps with a prostitute), instead of rationalizing away the misdeed, don't forgive him. Once you allow a lover to get away with murder, he knows he can keep chipping away at your soul, inch by painful inch. Although Dave cooked Sheila lavish meals, this woman lived on crumbs.

Chapter 15

If You Need Drama, Rent a Movie

Rob Says

I was pretty monogamous during my relationship with Janie. I realize *pretty monogamous* is similar to *sort of pregnant* but I did the best I could at the time.

All my life I've tried to be nothing like my dad. He was an abusive drunk. My mom stuck it out with him for way too long.

Being a musician, it's never been difficult for me to attract women. I've had more than my share of rock groupies and strippers. Guess that's why the first thing that attracted me to Janie was her chest. We met at this bizarre private club owned by an aging Hollywood icon. It had some Mediterranean design with sand on the floor. The crowd was stereotypical L.A. Janie and I were the only two that admitted the scene that night was the most stupid in the world.

We became a couple very quickly. I moved into her place four months after we met. It was great to be with an intelligent, career-minded woman instead of a bimbo. We had a lot in common. What we didn't have was passion. I told myself great sex wasn't as important as all these other terrific things I shared with Janie. But what did I know about healthy relationships? I'd never been around one in my life.

Not that my relationship with Janie lacked its share of craziness. Janie is very easily offended by sex and has a narrow range of what she considers appropriate sexual behavior. Any variance from that range reminds Janie of her father, whom she considers the ultimate deviant. But from the specifics she's described about her upbringing—well, I just think Janie's dad liked to have a good time.

Now Janie's mom is truly a bitch. She stayed with us one Thanksgiving weekend and totally flipped out. There was an ugly scene. Janie was a full participant in helping to kick her mom out of our house. Later Janie had a guilt attack and blamed me for everything.

Anything that made Janie uncomfortable became my fault. At some point she started accusing me of being a sex addict. Now, every animal is addicted to sex. There's even a body of thought that says people can be compulsively drawn to sex, but that doesn't mean they're addicts. I'm not saying this to justify my cheating. But it wasn't like I was constantly tomcatting around. Including the occasional one-night stand, I had six affairs in our eight years together.

I proposed marriage because it seemed like after seven years together that's what you're supposed to do. I did the whole formal thing, bought the ring and got on my knee to pop the question. She said yes but made me sign a prenup.

Janie and I put together an amazing wedding. Again, we made a great team. But after the hoopla was over reality set in.

We were married and I could no longer just walk away from my wife or from the fact that we had problems together. I grew less tolerant of flaws in the relationship.

Around this time Janie and her therapist convinced me to take antidepressants. They made me less unhappy but also less happy—sort of flat. I stayed on the meds until after I walked out on Janie.

The marriage deteriorated in under a year. Jane caught me in chat rooms looking for raw passion, and got angry. I took off, hooked up with a stripper, and never looked back.

It was comfortable in lots of ways being with Janie. We had a nice lifestyle. I wasn't a kept man. Bills got split down the middle. But essentially for eight years I stayed with a woman who is the opposite of my ideal.

Did I love Janie? Sure, and my childhood dogs, too. I know that's sarcastic but I don't think I truly loved another being unconditionally until my daughter was born two years ago. Now that I know what love is, I can no longer justify lying to people in my life.

That's a lesson I learned too late to save my second marriage. Yes, I got hitched to a stripper. Right now I'm unattached and working as a recording engineer.

I feel bad about a lot of the things I did to Janie. But I'm not responsible for the choices she makes with her life. I'm trying to move on and break my patterns. She keeps winding up with guys who have different faces but the same MO.

Life teaches you the same lesson over and over 'til you get it. My baby taught me my lesson: Be honest.

Janie Says

The men I fall for are carbon copies of one another: losers who I hoped could be saved through the love of this good woman.

I couldn't save my dad, the sex addict. My parents broke up

after he had an affair with my sixteen-year-old baby sitter. My childhood memories include weekend visits at Dad's house listening to him having sex with strippers and prostitutes through paper-thin walls.

Professionally I've led a blessed life. I'm a successful film producer. But I'd never commission a movie about my love life, particularly my marriage. It would make such a cheesy flick.

I met my husband in 1989 when I was thirty. He was twenty-eight and fresh out of a drug and alcohol rehab program. Signs were present early on that Rob was a player. There was always a woman around, but he kept saying, "Oh, she's just a friend." During our first night together he admitted he had gonorrhea. Soon after it came out that he'd recently gotten three girls pregnant around the same time. One of them kept the baby but Rob refused to take any responsibility for his son's upbringing.

I've always put up with practically any "bad boy" behavior. That stems from my dad saying Mom was unbearable, that if she'd been *nice* he would have stayed married.

Rob put even my tolerance level to the test. The theme of our eight-year relationship was he'd do something awful, I'd yell, he'd blame me, *I'd* wind up apologizing!

Everything was drama. Rob would get a flat tire and have a *raging* meltdown way out of proportion to the reality of the situation. Once he snapped over who-remembers-what and flung a balled-up roll of socks so hard at a neon sign in our living room that the sign smashed into a million pieces. I'm lucky he never hit me.

He had a yo-yo day job and played rock music, so I viewed him as a struggling artist, not a loser. Whenever we went anywhere, I'd pay. When we decided to live together two years into the relationship, he broke speed records getting his meager belongings out of his dump and into my $3 million mansion.

That's when the extent of his womanizing began to surface. One afternoon I was on the treadmill and saw his American

Express bill on the table. I don't know why but I jumped off the machine and took a look. There was a charge listed for a Flamingo Hotel. The treadmill still running, I grabbed the phone book and found the address. In a trance, garbed in my workout clothes, I scooped up my car keys and, without even closing my front door, raced to the Flamingo. It was a Triple-X pleasure palace, the type with mirrors on the ceiling and king-sized water beds. For twenty minutes I sat in the parking lot watching gross, dirty men walking in and out of the entrance with young girls draped over them.

Rob's response when I confronted him with the results of my afternoon field trip was to fly into a rage, sweep all my novels off the bookshelves, and light into me for not trusting him. He claimed that he'd loaned his Amex card on the night in question to his friend John. I needed to believe him, so eventually I did.

A few weeks later we went to a party at the home of one of the Doobie Brothers. This girl I'd never met walked up to me and said, "Janie, you're the luckiest girl in the world. Rob's *some* hunk." Just as I was recovering from that, another girl walked up and said, "Do yourself a favor. Make him behave."

When we got home, I screamed at Rob, "What in the name of God are they talking about?"

He screamed back, "You're so paranoid. Why can't you ever trust me?"

Our fight that night was so bad he stormed out and didn't come home until the next morning. Still, I forgave him. Being a patsy was better than being *unbearable*.

No matter how unbearable Mom had been to my dad, she didn't deserve what I was about to do to her. It was November 1993. She'd just been diagnosed with breast cancer and wanted to spend Thanksgiving with Rob and me. Of course I said yes. Mom had always been a difficult person. Being sick made her angry at the world.

This resulted in over-the-top behavior. I'd say, "I'm gonna serve dinner in this room." She'd scream, "I *hate* that room."

Rob started laying into her: "You're crazy. You're unbearable. Get the fuck out of here." She screamed back.

I tried to appease everybody but the fight escalated. Rob went into the guest bedroom and started throwing my mother's clothes out the second-floor window. He then called 911 to say, "My girlfriend's mother is having a nervous breakdown. Get her out of here."

In the background the cops heard my mom sobbing hysterically, "You're killing me." Four squad cars pulled up to my driveway. Cops spilled out, guns drawn. The police took Rob and my mother away in separate cars.

My mom's last words to me for nearly a year were, "I pray my cancerous blood runs through your body and you die a miserable death."

Right after this episode Rob and I began couples counseling. The shrink quickly sized him up and said that to continue therapy with her, he had to join Sex Addicts Anonymous. She also recommended he take Zoloft, the happy pill. He did all this. It killed his sex drive but it also killed his temper.

It was impressive that he was willing to work so hard on our relationship. So at the end of 1994 we got engaged. My mom recovered from the cancer and actually gave me money for a bridal gown. She hated Rob but the brush with death made her value having a relationship with her daughter.

The wedding, a black-tie affair for four hundred was so lavish we made the style columns. But I spent that night sitting on the side of the bed crying.

Marriage soured the relationship for me. I had different expectations of a boyfriend than I did of a husband. Rob had always given 50 percent of himself emotionally and financially. Suddenly that didn't seem enough, even though Rob swore he was going to sign up for college classes and get a real career.

Rob signed the death warrant on the marriage when he went off Zoloft prior to having knee surgery, sank into a suicidal depression, and got addicted to cyber-porn.

The last *last* straw occurred the night we had a flat tire on the way to a Hollywood premiere. It took AAA so long to get to us that we missed the movie and didn't bother going to the after-party, just back home. All this put me in a foul mood, which wasn't helped by Rob trying once again to entice me to look at one of his favorite computer slut sites. I screamed at him to get out of the house, we were done.

Rob stayed out the whole night. That wasn't unusual but two days passed and he didn't show up or call. I finally had a cop friend track him down down. My husband was at a Flamingo-type hotel shacked up with a seventeen-year-old stripper. At the time Rob was thirty-six.

He moved in with the stripper and her nine-month-old son. Where was the baby's father? In Folsom prison. Rob told me, "This is the first relationship where I've felt like an equal."

Three months later they were kaput and he was back on my doorstep with flowers. Thank God I finally realized Rob wasn't the man I expected him to be. I told him to find another stripper, which he did. They married, had a child, and are in the process of divorcing.

I'm just coming off another relationship with a guy who has a fetish for strippers. A few weeks ago I filled out an application for a dating service. There was a blank after the question, "What have you learned from your previous relationships?" I wrote, "What you see is what you get. A person is who he is, not what you want him to be."

I have been in therapy on and off since the age of six. I've tried group, private counseling, and groups for the brokenhearted. I can tell you the egg my dysfunctional patterns crawled out of: being exposed to Dad and his prostitutes. I am counseled out. It's like a cancer victim who's had dose after dose of radiation. After a certain point you have to rely on your inner resources to heal. It's either that or die.

Sherry Says

There are couples who long for a love life that follows the plot of a romance novel: predictable, PC, and pothole free. Janie and Rob's story was the anti-Harlequin. There are no rose-colored glasses to diffuse the impact of this nontraditional, decidedly nonpretty story.

Janie and Rob were typical of those who fear that "typical" (traditional) relationships are boring. Their tale was certainly dramatic, but it's one that is more entertaining to watch than to live through.

Where Rob Erred

Rob compensated for Janie's overreliance on therapy with an underutilization of his God-given brain cells. Until recently, his approach to love was primitive, animalistic, and *totally* mindless. He saw someone he wanted and went for it, damn the consequences. He accepted no responsibility for getting one, two, three women pregnant. For a man whose life ambition was to be nothing like his abusive dad, he bore a stark resemblance to his parent.

On one level Rob knew his pursuit of sexy bimbos was unhealthy but couldn't quite figure out how to begin to develop relationship-building skills. A true receptivity to therapy might have been of benefit to this hurting and hurtful boy-man.

His semantic double-talk about the nature of sexual addiction was self-serving and basically unintelligible. His defense of the actions of Janie's father around his little girl (*he just liked to have a good time*) would be laughable if it weren't so awful.

Rob's constant cheating (*Pretty monogamous?* Pretty lame!), lying, and explosive outbursts were the actions of a callous coward. To storm out on his marriage and not even call his wife to inform her he was alive, albeit shacked up with a stripper, is beyond comment. Even after fatherhood helped Rob experience an "epiphany" that honesty and decency count, he couldn't acknowledge that his treatment of Janie's mother bordered on the criminal.

Where Rob Shone

Although a liar and compulsive cheater, Rob made it clear to Janie literally from the get-go exactly the type of egg from which he had crawled.

Rob freely admitted that he was clueless about the nature of healthy relationships and did try in his uneducated, limited way to build a life with Janie based not just on sex. The problem was he thought a relationship had to be either/or: All passion or zero passion.

Hopefully, now that he knows what love is, he can begin to treat himself and others lovingly.

Where Janie Erred

Despite *knowing the egg her dysfunctional patterns* crawled out of, Janie remains attached to a way of life that brings her drama, danger, and despair.

Rob is a normal woman's nightmare and a drama queen's dream man. The healthy response, upon meeting a man whom, in short order you discover has recently made three women pregnant and—oh yes, bonus prize—is infected with gonorrhea, would be to recoil in disgust.

Janie welcomed Rob into her arms and home, then flipped out each and every time her lover acted in an untrustworthy fashion. When he'd meet her accusation with a counter-offensive, she'd back down. Otherwise, in order to maintain her façade of self-respect, she'd have had to kick this crazy-making man out of her life. That wasn't an option: *Being a patsy was better than being unbearable.*

Regardless of whether she was a coconspirator in the Thanksgiving Day Massacre of 1993, allowing her sick mother to be hauled off in a squad car demonstrates the lowest depths to which a human can sink. It offers proof of Janie's total self-loathing. No one who respects herself could be party to such a nightmarish and inexcusable scene. The place to deal with rage at one's parent and unhealthy need to placate one's boyfriend is in therapy.

Obviously Janie shouldn't have stayed in her soulless pairing for eight minutes, much less for eight years. And how sad that when she did jump ship, she landed in the arms of a Rob clone.

As Janie, survivor of a stupendously traumatic childhood is aware, therapy is not a cure-all. While valuable, ultimately it's what she does during the hours *not* spent on the chair (or couch) that most impacts her ability to build a healthy lovestyle. It's far easier to stay mired in "victimhood", and keep having essentially the *same* relationship, than to make a real effort to change her behavior. If she overcomes those deep-seated patterns and still can't forge a lasting love, then all might seem truly hopeless. That's an utterly frightening proposition for her to contemplate. So she protects herself by burrowing back to known ways of behaving.

This may be safe but it's self-destructive in the long term. A practical versus psychiatric approach is to "retrain her brain" to stop it from rushing into those well-worn grooves when faced with familiar stimuli. For example, the next time Janie meets a man with an apparent stripper fetish, she should stop and note her desire to rush into his arms. Then immediately think of something else, for example the misery that inevitably awaits her if she follows through on her desire. Or about what a fun time she had at the premiere of her latest movie. Or how great it will feel to be curled up in front of a fire with a trustworthy, nurturing man who would never dream of calling the cops on her sick mom.

True, it takes time to undertake behavioral modification of this magnitude. And much, much effort. But so does rushing into certain misery time and time again. The difference is that one endeavor brings her pain and the other might eventually bring her lasting passion.

Where Janie Shone

Given the extent of the emotional damage Janie endured at the hands of her parental "role models," the fact that she has forged a successful professional life and still attempts to create a fulfilling personal one is testament to the survival instincts of human beings.

Your Love Lesson From This Couple's Breakup

There are the usual Rashamonesque divides in this story. Rob believes he and Janie moved in together after a few months, and that he continued taking Zoloft until after the marital split. Janie insists they didn't officially live together for two years, and that the marital split was partially caused by Rob's going off the Zoloft.

This couple was doomed to fail. They were both emotionally damaged, not cognizant of what it took to build a healthy relationship, and addicted to living in constant turmoil.

My Biggest Heartbreak and What It Taught Me About Love

Gary James, 43, police officer

My marriage of twelve years broke up for a variety of reasons. Finances were rocky, I worked the graveyard shift in Homicide, and communication and intimacy between my wife and me had reached a level that was dangerously low. The relationship gradually deteriorated and counseling couldn't stem the tide. My ex would have been content to stay together despite her unhappiness because the marriage represented a certain level of security for her.

Once I finally left I dissolved into a puddle of loneliness and guilt over leaving my two small daughters. To avoid being alone I quickly escaped into a relationship with a woman so self-centered my kids came to call her Cruella DeVil.

When that relationship ended a few years later, I finally began mourning my marriage. Despite my having been the one to call it quits, there was a lot of grief. What followed for me was a year and a half period where I didn't date but devoted myself to intense soul searching. I not only forgave my ex for her mistakes; I forgave myself for leaving. I didn't expect her to forgive me, however. I accepted that she blamed me for the divorce. Just like when we were married, everything negative was my fault. That's her feeling and she's entitled to it.

Despite our differences, my ex and I have managed to put the needs of our children first. I tell the girls to be respectful of their mother's new boyfriend, and instead of dwelling on the high number I have to write on the child support checks I tell myself I'm providing for the two people I cherish most in the world.

It took us five years but my ex and I have moved to a new plateau of friendship and caring. Divorce wasn't an end but a new beginning.

Chapter 16

Two Half-People Don't Make One Whole

Suzanne Says

There were two reasons I married Barry. First, I didn't want to hurt the feelings of a handicapped person. He'd had a colostomy, and for the rest of his life had to relieve himself into a bag. Secondly, marriage seemed like the only way I could escape my dysfunctional family.

My parents had a horrible relationship. Three blocks from the house I'd hear them yelling at each other. I never saw any affection between them . . . or toward me. My father hugged me for the first time two years ago.

I grew up with low self-esteem and was fearful of everything from bugs to heights. I was pretty, so my only source of power was my sexuality.

I had tons of boyfriends and lost my virginity in 1965, at age fifteen. Two years later I was a freshman and pinned to a frat boy who owned a hot, white sports car with a red interior. I'd heard about the saga of Barry and his ulcer long before he and I actually met. When we were finally introduced, I noticed his emaciated body topped by a sad, beautiful smile.

He kept asking me out and I kept saying I was pinned. Barry started sending me telegrams, each containing one line of a sonnet. The final couplet arrived with an ultimatum: Go out with me or the sonnets stop here. My heart was moved. We started dating and eventually decided to get married. We had a long engagement and I guess a part of me thought the wedding day would never really arrive.

This was the era of free sex. The president of the student council and I were having an affair. The morning of my wedding I took him to the honeymoon suite of the Plaza, which Barry and I had rented for that night.

I don't remember having sex with Barry that day. What I do remember is weeping in the bathtub a few hours before the wedding, desperately unhappy at the thought of marrying my fiancé. My mother said every bride got nervous and that it was way too late to back out.

At the reception, during our first dance, Barry whispered into my ear that he'd quit his job as a junior copywriter and wanted to devote himself to being a poet. This became a theme during our marriage: He never brought in money. And he never informed me about major life decisions that would affect both of us—until after the fact.

In the decades since this marriage ended, I've developed a consciousness and have metamorphosed into a spiritual, caring human being. But in those days, I was a terrible person. One example: I had to force myself to have sex with my husband. Yet, I took a course called Problems in Marriage and screwed the professor.

Barry got a job teaching freshman English at a small college in

Oregon. Once there, I can't tell you how many affairs I had behind my husband's back. One of my flings made me pregnant. Barry thought it was his baby but supported my decision to have an abortion.

Soon after we moved to Iowa so Barry could go for his MFA (Masters in Fine Arts). I enrolled in grad school. My goal was to teach art therapy to handicapped kids. I also worked as a barmaid, cocktail waitress, at a ketchup factory, and as a teacher's assistant. People around campus knew me as "Suzanne Flower Person" because I sold daisies off a cart. The goal of all these jobs was to score enough money to buy pot and acid.

Barry's drug of choice was Quaaludes. These are as powerful and addictive as heroin. It became *impossible* to communicate with my constantly wasted husband, who had very long hair, wore makeup, and wrote manifestos about art.

In a quirk of fate Barry introduced me to a faculty member who became the love of my life. Richard was a novelist from France who was very talented and very married. We fell into a mad affair that lasted for years.

I do recall sleeping with Barry around this period, although my husband wouldn't touch me unless he was convinced our union would be spiritual. I considered the sex more kinky than spiritual because Barry had me put on a blonde wig and pretend I was someone else.

I got pregnant—this time by Richard. Again, Barry thought it was his, and again pressed me to get rid of the baby. My mother said I wasn't ready for parenthood and set up an abortion for me back home. I didn't want to end the pregnancy but I listened to both of them and had the operation. This was the last time I allowed myself to be pushed into doing something I didn't want to do. The abortion haunts me still.

No longer pregnant, I stepped back into the role of stoned hippie wife. Since Barry and I constantly had company it was natural to invite Richard and his wife, Gina, over for spaghetti and meatballs.

During dinner Richard stood up and said, "I love Suzanne. I can't be without her." It was like a bomb exploded in the room. Gina dragged her husband out the door. I spent the night in a hotel.

The next day I went to Richard's farmhouse. Gina said he'd taken off for Mexico. She added I wasn't his first tramp and I wouldn't be the last, although most of them were younger than me. I was twenty-two. She then leapt at me and scratched my face.

She cut me in another way by sleeping with Barry. Obviously it was all about revenge. It worked: I was enraged.

Barry and I worked on the marriage, hopeless as it was. We moved again. As usual I supported us with a variety of odd jobs while my husband labored over his art. He made our apartment into a performance space, labeling everything, then inviting people over for a viewing. I was "sleeping nude."

Richard was now living in California and contacted my parents to find out my telephone number. I wired him money to visit me.

I remember waiting for Richard outdoors during a blizzard. He never showed up. Snow fell around me and my heart split open. I came home and told Barry we had to end the marriage. I still loved Richard.

Barry left and I leaned against the door, overwhelmed with relief. It felt like being released from jail.

This marriage represented who I was in my young, powerless phase. If I hadn't left Barry I'd have stayed a little girl who constantly acted out but never took concrete, positive action.

I married Barry out of compassion for his condition. Ironically I hurt him throughout the marriage by being unfaithful.

I was thirty-three when I met my current husband. Aaron offers me the ultimate form of love by allowing me to be who I am without compromise. He doesn't try to mold or change me, nor I him.

I could never have built that sort of relationship in my twenties. Young couples are still trying to establish themselves as individuals. Consequently their relationship often degenerates into power struggles.

Who I am in a relationship is reflective of where I am in my personal development. Now that I'm a good person I can be a good partner.

Barry Says

It was Suzanne's boots that first got my attention—they were high—practically to her panty line, black, and high-heeled. Very sexy. I don't recall who initiated the first contact in the college cafeteria but I remember us exchanging several intrigued looks.

I was only twenty when we met, but I'd had lots of girlfriends. My parents' relationship was loving and loyal. Consequently I've always tended toward monogamy. I very much wanted to start my own family.

There was an immediate physical attraction between Suzanne and me, as well as a profound spiritual connection. And she was very supportive of my aspirations, helping me put together a literary magazine for the college.

We both lived at home. My mother, who was pretty progressive, would give me money so I could take Suzanne to a hotel for some privacy.

I have a hazy memory of proposing to Suzanne on bended knee in her parents' basement eleven months after we met. I gave her my grandmother's engagement ring, a beautiful cut diamond. Much later we hocked that ring to pay bills.

After a yearlong engagement Suzanne and I had a big, traditional Jewish wedding. We spent our first night together as man and wife in the honeymoon suite at the Plaza. It was a perfect beginning to what my young, romantic self assumed would be a perfect relationship.

We were little kids playing house. I had a romantic vision of a wife who would support me while I made my way as a poet. Suzanne was pretty good about this but not having money gets in the way of happiness.

Suzanne and I left our first home and retreated to the safe world of academia. At school I noticed Suzanne doing a lot of flirting. I did, too, but it never crossed my mind to carry it further. I think it crossed Suzanne's mind.

I didn't have enough confidence that I could make my wife happy. When I felt weak I acted strong. I don't think Suzanne knew the real me versus the façade. It didn't help that I was constantly stoned. I took the drugs to mask my growing unhappiness.

Our spiritual connection stemmed from an appreciation of the poetry I was writing. I noticed Suzanne disconnecting. She had no idea what to do with her life other than be pretty and supportive of her husband the artist. Her solution to filling in the blanks was to have affairs.

She fell for a visiting writer from Paris. He was an alcoholic, married with five kids. I found out about the affair in a terrible way. The phone rang. Suzanne answered it, then told me to pick up. Richard had something very important to tell me. The "something" was that he and my wife were in love. I was flabbergasted. I'd considered him my friend so this was a double betrayal.

I was shaking in my shoes. Suzanne and I went to Richard's house to talk some more. She came home with me, I think. My recollections are a bit hazy. I'm sure I was stoned.

Soon after things took an even more soap-operaish turn. Suzanne became pregnant. She said it was mine but I was never sure. I'd always wanted a child but not under these circumstances so it made sense to end the pregnancy.

While Suzanne was having an abortion, the novelist's wife and I slept together. I told Suzanne when she returned. That had been the point—to upset my wife.

Somehow we bounced back. She assured me the affair with Richard was over. Around this period we did some sexual experimenting with another couple. These drug-induced incidents were antithetical to my true monogamous nature. Looking back, I'm disgusted at my behavior.

I completed my MFA in poetry. Suzanne took a series of temp jobs. I had a part-time job in Bloomingdale's arts and books department.

We coexisted. I felt tired, suspicious and jealous. The marriage was scarred. This tension didn't help our sex life.

Six months after coming back home, five years after we got together, Suzanne came home with a black eye. She said Richard was in town, they'd been together, and he had hit her.

I became hysterical, completely irrational. I grabbed my Chihuahua and took off.

This was the first time either of us had ever lived alone. I drove a cab for awhile then moved to Europe for a year where I lived out another bohemian fantasy. I never became Jack Kerouac. I make my living as an art dealer but I'll write poetry 'til the day I die.

Once my anger and bitterness faded I was able to take a lot of responsibility for the failure of the marriage. We essentially sowed our wild oats together and shared a spiritual connection centered in our mutual love of art. Suzanne carried it a bit far: Getting attracted to *other* writers wasn't part of the deal.

My immaturity and the drugs clouded everything. I didn't pay attention to Suzanne during our marriage or think about what she needed. I don't think my current wife would recognize the man-child I was during my first marriage.

It's not necessarily a good thing to marry your first love. You need to get certain things out of your system before settling down, to get over possessively feeling your partner belongs to you and that her actions should revolve around fulfilling her needs.

If Suzanne and I had met later in life I think we'd have had a shot at making it as a couple. As it is, I count her among my closest friends.

Punch/Counterpunch

BARRY: I found out about Suzanne's affair when Richard called to say he was in love with my wife.

SUZANNE: During dinner Richard stood up and told Barry, "I love Suzanne. I can't be without her."

SUZANNE: I had two abortions. In both cases Barry believed he was the father. He was wrong both times.

BARRY: Suzanne got pregnant once during our marriage. I doubted that I was the father.

BARRY: Suzanne came home sporting a black eye. She said she'd been with Richard, still madly loved him, and that our marriage was over.

SUZANNE: Richard stood me up in a blizzard. I came home and told Barry our marriage was over.

Sherry Says

At eighteen one is deemed legally able to wed. Unfortunately that significant landmark rarely coincides with an emotional readiness to pledge eternal troth to a fellow or female partner. There is no age at which drug-taking is sanctioned.

Young, confused, and more than a tad heedless, Suzanne and Barry's unspoken wedding vows read: "We promise to love, honor, and sow wild oats together. . . ." I don't usually get biblical but as you sow so shall you reap.

Where Suzanne Erred

A lack of self-esteem coupled with a surplus of self-absorption led Suzanne to make a series of uber-serious blunders. Ruled by these seemingly antithetical impulses, she dated and subsequently married Barry for a plethora of frighteningly wrong-headed reasons. None of which had anything to do with her feelings toward her husband.

Yes, pity was in the mix. Feeling herself to be unworthy of happiness, her mind-set was: *Why shouldn't I be a vessel of joy to the unfortunate?* Another factor edging her toward unholy matrimony was a desire to be the center of another person's universe: *If I matter to someone else, consequently I matter in the world.* Certainly marriage seemed a great way to escape her dysfunctional home environment. Primarily, however, Suzanne joined herself to Barry because her decision-making style lacked decisiveness. Avoidance, rather than reasoning ruled her world: *Instead of thinking through whether I should marry a man I don't love, I'll take a joint and/or a sex partner.*

Her life remained in drift mode throughout the marriage. If panic and pain threatened to percolate toward consciousness past the many fuzzy layers of her brain, she'd anesthetize it with the usual "fixes." She tumbled into the nadir of self-destructiveness when she allowed herself to be talked into an unwanted abortion.

Should she have felt remorse at the multiple betrayals of her husband? Should she have helped him face and kick his drug addiction? Yes, and yes, but if a person can't keep herself afloat, how can she prevent someone else from sinking?

Where Suzanne Shone

She wasn't heartless, just oblivious of her humanity as well as that of her husband. This stoned hippie wife often traveled the extra mile in her efforts to be supportive of her man, doing everything from moving cross-country and acting as sole breadwinner to participating in Barry's art efforts.

Where Barry Erred

This poor schnook was married, not to a flesh-and-blood woman but to the poetic notion of love everlasting. He hadn't clue one as to what marriage in the real world entailed.

While claiming to share a profound spiritual bond with his wife, Barry rarely attempted to communicate with Suzanne in a manner that verged beyond the superficial. His self-imposed deceptions began early in the relationship. How else to explain his belief that Suzanne not only loved him, but loved jumping his bones? The reality: Suzanne spent the afternoon of her wedding having sex with another man in the honeymoon suite she'd rented with Barry, then weeping at the prospect of her upcoming nuptials. Her oblivious bridegroom proclaimed their wedding night to be *a perfect beginning to what my young, romantic self assumed would be a perfect relationship.*

Barry's priority was his art. He expected his wife to put food on the table even if the only way she could do so was by hocking her engagement ring. Additionally, he expected his wife to put on a blonde wig and pretend to be someone else during intercourse, clothing his kinky desires in a proclamation that what the couple shared was spiritual sex. And he made little or no effort to help Suzanne discover if she had any other aspirations in his life other than being the woman behind the man.

Barry was stoned during most of the marriage, which makes it *nearly* forgivable that he only recalls Suzanne undergoing one abortion. Quaaludes or no Quaaludes, he should have realized how strongly his wife wanted a baby. As for his one-night stand with Richard's wife, it's not his proudest moment but it is an understandable move on the part of a cuckolded husband.

Where Barry Shone

He had a forgiving nature and a willingness not to give up at the first sign of trouble. However, he was deluding himself after the many signs of trouble that Suzanne clearly showed him.

Your Love Lesson From This Couple's Breakup

When they met Barry and Suzanne were each like lumps of clay. Their personalities were that ill-defined. What they had in common were feelings of insecurity, fear, loneliness, and a cluelessness about what life was about. These are reasons for therapy, not marriage. Two lost souls have to find themselves rather than clutch at each other.

Chapter 17

Always Right? Think Again

Al Says

What drew me to Ronni was her strong desire to start a family. I guess that's why we married ten weeks after first clapping eyes on each other.

My parents were Jewish refugees from Poland. They met in New York City after World War II. Their relationship wasn't idyllic—Mom was *definitely* the dominant figure—but they stayed together fifty-six years and raised two kids.

I married at twenty-three, thinking my wife Beth and I would raise a family and be together for life. Four years later Beth suddenly announced she felt trapped and was leaving. This stunned me. She was in grad school, studying psychology. How could she make *no* effort to work things out?

Six months after the split I got involved with a woman who made it clear she never wanted children. We were together for seven years, until I traveled to Seattle to work on a business venture.

That's where I met Ronni. She was another displaced Easterner. Our initial dinner together lasted six hours then we moved to a coffee shop for more conversation. That first night we talked about having children. It appealed to her that I was a lawyer, a good provider, and it made me happy that she wanted to be a homemaker and concentrate on raising a family.

Although I felt less raw physical attraction toward Ronni than in my previous two relationships, things were sexually exciting. Plus, she was a real helpmate in getting my fledgling business deal off the ground. During a vacation in Denver to visit her brother, Ronni suggested getting married. I went to a pay phone and called the local government office to check the legalities, and we did the deed.

Two months later, according to plan, Ronni was pregnant. After our son was born, we moved back east and bought a one hundred and fifty-year-old country house in the suburbs complete with white picket fence.

Over a nine-year period Ronni was either pregnant or postpregnant so sex tailed off. Frankly, she began losing interest in sex and/or in me while carrying our first child.

I was present for the birth of all three of our children and also for an induced abortion Ronni had to undergo after the fetus died inside her body. I thought these shared experiences were powerful enough to bond us for life.

The focus of our existence was on parenting. We backed each other up so the children could never play one parent against the other. None of the kids ever caused a problem. They were a *tremendous* source of satisfaction and went a long way toward compensating me for the lack of passion.

Boy, was there a lack. It got to the point where Ronni and I made love just a few times a year. Some people may not be into sex but they're at least touchy-huggy. Ronni's physical style is not affectionate. She wouldn't even hold my hand.

Certainly I was attracted to other women but for many years I didn't allow myself to go beyond fantasizing. In the early 80s Ronni and I went for marital counseling to deal with this issue but nothing changed.

Other problems developed. Ronni was programmed to have intense conflicts with someone in order to be happy. For years, she had disputes with her family. Then my mother—who admittedly has serious shortcomings—did something Ronni regarded as an unforgivable slight. I initially sided with Ronni but eventually I let my mother back into my life. I mean, she's the woman who birthed me! My wife accused me of abandoning her.

Ronni did a lot of stuff that was crazy. Our then-fourteen-year-old son wanted to visit my sister. Hating my family as she does, Ronni threatened the boy, "If you go to your horrible aunt against my wishes, I'll never speak to you again." I told the boy to ignore his mother and do as he pleased. Predictably, Ronni eventually calmed down. Also true to form she never apologized for her outburst.

When our youngest was six, Ronni expressed discontentment at being a full-time mom. We'd moved into the city and she began getting involved in community projects. This was a great outlet for her energies and talents but she became less interested in parenting. In the evenings around 8 P.M. she'd say, "I just *have* to get out of here," call a friend, and dash out the door.

I filled in the slack on the homefront, but started questioning the basis of our marriage. If you took away our shared devotion to the children, what was there? To find out and to deal with the no-sex stalemate I suggested we again try therapy. She refused.

This was *very* frustrating to me. I had no interest in cheating. I wanted sex in the context of a loving relationship but suddenly all my repressed desires swam to the surface. I found myself obsessing about my female clients. I told Ronni, "If things don't improve, I'm going to start dating other women."

She responded, "If that's what you want to do, go ahead." Obviously my wife didn't care one way or the other what I did.

I wasn't secretive about my attempts to meet women. Ronni's reactions ranged from annoyance to disinterest. I began seeing someone who after a few dates said, "I'm not getting involved with a married man. Leave your wife and then we'll be together."

Ronni finally took seriously what was going on after I informed her I was moving out. She begged me to change my mind and handed me a book that chronicled the negative effects of divorce on children. One morning, really early before the kids woke up, huddled in the kitchen I promised my wife that I'd stay. We hugged.

Unfortunately Ronni didn't subsequently act like we'd weathered a major crisis. This was astounding to me. She still had no regard for my need for sex and affection. Nevertheless, I stopped dating the other woman and recommitted myself to the marriage.

At this point we owned two adjoining apartments in our building. One was our home, the other my office. Ronni and I discussed starting a fast-food business together. She'd generate and design the menus; I'd handle the business side. She never followed up. It really hurt me to watch my wife go full-steam ahead working on other projects but never follow through on our proposed undertaking.

Two years later—two years of faithfulness—I again issued Ronni an ultimatum: Make a change in how you treat me or I'm gone. It wouldn't have taken massive amounts of sex to get me to stay. We felt good as a couple. We'd raised nice kids together. But Ronni didn't even have the desire to fake it. I got the impression that her being physically affectionate with me would feel morally degrading.

I began dating the woman I now live with, and moved into the adjoining apartment. Because I was so close by it took our eight-year-old two weeks to realize Mommy and Daddy had split up. Ronni threw my clothes out into the hall a few times but I did my level best to keep any nasty scenes out of eye- and earshot of the children.

After six years apart we're still legally separated. I have no intention of going back to Ronni. It just seemed easier to continue supporting my family and not put settlement numbers down on paper. But my girlfriend is pressuring me to get a divorce.

These days Ronni's violent temper is primarily directed at her sister, who is now working as my assistant. In spite of the fact that it was Ronni's idea for Gena to come work for me!

I gave the marriage my best shot. If Ronni weren't so self-absorbed we'd never have split up. But I've recently come to discover through analysis that I may have contributed to some of the problems. I always saw myself as the giving guy and Ronni as the one who was so focused on what she viewed as my physical imperfections that she couldn't see the beauty right in front of her eyes.

Ronni Says

For close to twenty years Al refused to do the one thing I swore would make me want to sleep with him. I'd beg him and beg him to clean up his act—to shower on a regular basis, comb his hair, and most of all lose the gut. He rarely failed to disappoint me.

That's been a familiar theme in my life: loved ones disappointing me. During my teens my parents divorced. A few years later they admitted that my "dad" wasn't my biological father. He'd married my mother when she was pregnant with me.

At twenty-four I married an English professor thirteen years my senior. He was the smartest person I'd ever met but almost immediately after the wedding he started sleeping with a bunch of his female students. If this had been my second marriage I might have been more cosmopolitan about the situation. At the time I found his cheating thoroughly unacceptable. We split after two years.

Next, I had a long relationship with a guy for whom I gave up my seven-room rent-controlled apartment so we could move out west and forge careers as illustrators. He thanked me for this sacrifice by sleeping with my best friend.

That's when I met Al. All the elements seemed in place. He was smart, interesting, the sex was good, and he wanted a family. Al liked to say that we met, married, and had our first child within a year.

He was terrific to talk to, very understanding, helpful, and a great father. However, what entered into the equation was that my boyish-looking, slender husband started to get fat. Actually, the flab centered on his midsection. He developed a *disgusting* stomach. I mean, the man popped out of his clothes. When Al started working from home he became a total slob: no longer showering on a regular basis, sitting down at the computer in the same shirt he'd slept in. I'm not talking about elaborate primping but a lack of basic hygiene!

I made it clear that Al's lack of cleanliness repulsed me. His arrogant attitude to my discomfort was: *Take me as I am*. It's not that Al wasn't a good, sensitive lover but I had to close my eyes in order to touch him.

Then Al got it into his head that we should be business partners. He never realized that spending 24/7 together made him even *less* attractive to me. Sex tailed off to once a month.

The other issue that divided us was his mother. She was a German refugee who'd lost many loved ones to the Nazis. During the best of times she treated me like a war criminal trying to infiltrate her family unit. The only time Al took my side over hers was immediately after the birth of our third child. As she did every Sunday, she ordered us to her house for dinner. Al said, "Ronni is nursing. Since she can't come over, I can't either." She got hysterical. *I was a horrible person. How could Al let me keep him from his real family?*

Growing up, my mom constantly criticized me. So it's disturbing and hurtful for me to have family conflicts. I will do everything to avoid them and let bygones be bygones. But Al's mother and I were now at war. She even stopped inviting me to Sunday dinner. After a while Al started visiting her without me. Despite my husband's total disregard for my feelings I opted for family harmony. For example, Al's sister is a lowlife, yet I've allowed my children to have relationships with her.

Al and I tried therapy once for a brief period but he was so rigid on our two divisive issues that it was ineffectual.

As the kids got older, Al urged me to get involved on the community board. He suggested this with the knowledge that meetings would take me out of the home several nights a week. I appreciated his support of my career. Consequently, unless there was a work-related reason I stuck close to home.

One day he gave me an ultimatum: *Start sleeping with me or I'm going to look for sex somewhere else.* As per usual, he refused to acknowledge I had a legitimate reason for not wanting him to touch me. I got very upset. We even went on vacation together a few times. I vaguely recall his going on a couple of dates but he quickly backed down on his threat and things went back to normal.

Two years later he gave me another ultimatum. I cried and carried on but to no avail. He became involved with a woman who is god-awful looking. She's a bleached blonde with horsey features, a head taller and years older than Al. It's pitiful that he cares so little about himself that he'd get involved with such a creature.

I felt horrible when he moved out—especially because he was

right next door! His selfishness and arrogance led him to rub my face in this miserable situation. Instead of ringing the bell, Al kept walking into my apartment at all hours, unannounced. I put a deadbolt lock on the door. He got in a rage and smashed the lock, in the process smashing the metal door. I replaced the lock and he smashed it again! Did he ever apologize to his children for carrying on like a madman in their earshot? Ha! The man has always been incapable of saying "I'm sorry."

Al doesn't want me anymore yet he has a sick need to be connected to my family. He asked my sister to work for him—an offer she accepted after I repeatedly *begged* her not to betray me. Al has dragged his heels over initiating a divorce. Clearly he wants the best of all possible worlds.

I married Al for the right reasons. He's basically a responsible, caring, decent man. When we met, I found him attractive. If Al had continued striving to meet my physical requirements, he'd be my ideal man for eternity. If it weren't for his arrogance and rigid attitude, we would still be together.

Punch/Counterpunch

AL: True to form, she never apologized for her outburst.
RONNI: Did he ever apologize? No.

AL: She had no regard for my need for sex and affection.
RONNI: For close to twenty years Al refused to do the one thing that would make me want to sleep with him.

RONNI: If it weren't for his arrogance and rigid attitude we would still be together.
AL: If Ronni weren't so self-absorbed we'd never have split up.

Sherry Says

Are these two peas in a pod or what? Ronni and Al were mirror images of each other. The trouble was that both viewed their own images as perfect.

When a couple's love dynamic is, "I'm right; you're wrong," they're both wrong.

Where Al Erred

Wedding a woman ten weeks after learning of her existence is not a typical recipe for marital happiness. However, after his first two serious relationships—both born of passion—derailed, Al changed his focus. He began hunting for the mother of his future children rather than for the love of his life. He should have been hunting for both.

Al's major boo-boo was that while he could recite chapter and verse on Ronni's shortcomings, the book was closed when it came to admitting any of his own. It's true that Ronni married him for better for worse/in fatness or in thinness. It's also true that Al should have made a sincere effort to be as attractive to her as possible. Daily showers and maintaining basic fitness don't seem like impossible requests to make of a spouse.

Nor does it seem like an impossible request for a wife to make of a husband that he put her needs before those of his mother. (Although probably the only man in Al's position who could satisfy the two women in question was named Solomon.) And it was misguided of Al to expect a wife who was cold toward him on her good days to buy into the romantic notion that the couple that works together stays together.

Where Al Shone

He was an excellent father, caring partner, and great provider . . . basically a super-dependable guy. You'd never read about this husband being caught snorting coke with a prostitute at 3 A.M. in some dive. To Al, sexual frustration was a small price to pay for the satisfactions of creating a stable family unit. This was not a man with commitment issues. He was in the relationship for the long haul—willing to put up with the good, the bad, and the ugly. His frustrations with his wife didn't prevent him from urging Ronni to utilize her talents and energies outside the home. While Al did eventually cheat on Ronni, he did it with due notice and intense provocation.

For the most part this husband kept his marital bargain: to keep the focus on parenting.

Where Ronni Erred

Ronni is unafraid of voicing strong negative opinions: *Al's sister is a lowlife. He became involved with a woman who is god-awful looking. Al developed a disgusting stomach.* Ronni's mule-headed method for dealing with her husband's intransigence over, among other things, that disgusting stomach: *It's my way or the highway.*

To wit, while she was well within her rights as a wife to express to her husband ways in which he might increase his sexual allure, she might have had better success from purring requests rather than barking orders. (*I made it clear that Al's lack of cleanliness repulsed me.*) More examples of her either/or mind-set: She viewed Al's need to maintain a connection with his parents, no matter how tenuous, as a repudiation of his wife.

Ronni's inability to widen by even a jot her understanding of Al's viewpoint sprang from her expectation of betrayal. (*A famil-*

iar theme in my life is loved ones disappointing me.) Such deep-rooted expectations often lead to a self-fulfilling prophecy. That is, doing everything in your power not to heal the breach causes a greater gulf. The unconscious thinking can go like this: *If I really open myself and my lover shuts down, then I'm a failure. If I stay closed, then its okay if the result is nothing ventured, nothing gained.*

What we have here is a fear of risk-taking.

Where Ronni Shone

Al freely admitted that Ronni was an excellent mother and in most respects, a wonderful wife. It's clear that when she was good (at homemaking, parenting, helping her husband establish himself as a lawyer), she was very, very good. And when she was bad . . .

Your Love Lesson From This Couple's Breakup

Notwithstanding the breakneck pace at which these two became a committed couple, they had a lot going for them. True, Al and Ronni ultimately couldn't pull together as a couple but when there was a shared goal (i.e., parenting happy, healthy children) they were a bang-up team.

Sadly, they also shared a stubborn pride that prevented them from making the slightest movement toward each other's rigid positions. Although both were hungry to be loved unconditionally, they continued to feel rebuffed time and again by the other's demands. This sense of rejection led to more stubbornness, alienation, distance and eventual separation.

Once the gloves were off and all pretense at "resolving" conflicts dropped, conflicts became viewed through pride and pain-blinded eyes. Ronni felt Al unilaterally chose his mother over his wife; he insisted Ronni was programmed to instigate family conflicts. She would swear to the death that she begged Al not to cheat on her; Al believed his decision to date left his wife unruffled. She accused him of asking her sister to be his assistant; he said the job offer was his estranged wife's idea. Both accused the other of initiating violent arguments in front of the children.

Each scored TKOs but neither won a jot of satisfaction. Their mutual rigidity helped them achieve a lose/lose scenario.

Sloan & George

Relationship b: 1982; d: 1992

Chapter 18

Don't Expect a Narcissist to be Capable of Anything More Than a *Ménage à Moi*

Sloan Says

I'm similar to Liz Taylor because I've had seven serious relationships in my life. I'm different from Liz Taylor because I didn't marry the men involved. It's not the government's place to sanction my love life.

George was serious relationship number four. The first time I laid eyes on him was at a Baltimore health club in December 1982. I was twenty-eight. A mutual friend introduced us figuring that George and I, both being artists, would have a lot in common. I considered myself a photographer/writer. George was a world-renowned portrait painter and sculptor—6'4" and reed-thin.

At the time, George was cultivating an androgynous look replete with shaved eyebrows and magenta lipstick. This appealed to me because although I looked like the apple-cheeked girl on the Sunmaid raisin box, inside I was totally punk. Along with his artistic nature George had a jubilant sense of life I found totally captivating.

It turned out that George and I lived on the same block and both made our holiday gifts from scratch. Another thing we had in common: Our conservative families considered us a little kooky. I want to stress, however, that my folks were always supportive and loving of their slightly "odd" daughter.

I loved George at first sight and after meeting him immediately ended a relationship with a married boyfriend. No, he wasn't one of the serious seven. George reacted to my passion by backing away. He still carried scars from having had his heart broken by a girlfriend in high school, and had steeled himself from needing anyone. Ever since, he'd start falling in love, then run. Four months after we met, he ran from me.

This made me terribly sad but I told George to take all the time he needed. It seemed pointless to carry on and throw verbal daggers like, "How dare you leave?" I wanted George to know I believed in him and understood his inner struggles. To me, love isn't about ensnaring someone in my web, but giving him the strength to be the best self possible.

Four months later, on the day a photo exhibit of mine opened at a local gallery, George called. He'd been in a skydiving accident, bumped his head, and was suddenly mad about me.

And so it began. Although we were together ten years George and I never shared a home. When couples live together they're in one space duking it out over physical and psychological territory. George and I would work all day in our separate lofts, meet at the gym, have dinner, take a nap, be intimate, then each return to work.

This system worked happily for us. We began running a party entertainment business together and joked that if we made it to thirteen years we'd have a bar and bat mitzvah to declare ourselves man and woman.

George and I ran into trouble over the issue of having kids. Although I wasn't in a rush to become a mother, it was something I definitely wanted. George was ambivalent about fatherhood but agreed to try for a baby. It turned out he had what the fertility specialists we eventually consulted called low sperm mobility.

Another big wrinkle: George was prone to having affairs. I'd be able to discern his infidelity because he would suddenly be extremely critical of things I was doing. This was *very* upsetting. Since I didn't regard George as my property I tried to bear the dismal situation with grace. I'd assure him of my love and ask, "Is there something I'm doing that isn't fulfilling you? Tell me who the woman is and what the affair means for us." My fear, which I shared with George, was that we'd walk into a party and I'd watch him share a conspiratorial wink with a woman. He'd invariably cry, "I didn't realize how much you mean to me, Sloan. I'll end the relationship."

He would and we'd go on, but I'd know in my heart that if *I* ever had an affair it would mean the beginning of the end for George and me. Because my affair wouldn't be about having my ego stroked, but about love.

Seven years into the relationship I developed deep feelings for another man, a friend of George's. This happened while George was in India, as it later turned out—becoming involved with another woman.

The fabric of us as a duo was obviously unraveling. But George and I possessed an ability to talk about anything and negotiate our way through hurdles that would have crushed other couples.

We rebuilt the foundation, but there were cracks. I experienced an increasing desire to move to New York, coupled with an increasing dissatisfaction with having a partner who was always half looking around for someone better. George loved the adventure of falling in love. And his narcissistic worldview made it difficult for him to ever put me first. For example, if I wanted to invite people to join us for dinner I couldn't trust that he'd be in the mood for company. Mostly, I grew tired of his need to focus on what he regarded as my flaws rather than at the big picture of all the wonderful things we shared together.

I took a sublet in New York and started shuttling back and forth between the two cities. George and I made plans to dissolve our business. We also started to dissolve personally—but there was no nastiness.

George met a woman who was "a kindred spirit." Yet he still spent that New Year's Eve with me. Through all this we kept semitrying to have a child.

We never stopped caring for each other. We stopped having the same goals. It takes more love to support the person in moving on than it does to try to glue him to your side. If you stay together you'll inflict tremendous pain. Even the most emotionally advanced people can reach the point where it's difficult not to attempt coercing their lover into acting a certain way.

George helped give me the confidence to grow in new directions. I'd say something funny, he'd laugh and insist, "Write that down. It's really funny." I wound up becoming a stand-up comic.

After our breakup, we had different sexual partners yet continued living a complementary existence. It's tough to give up the familiarity you share with someone after spending years together. So when George, who by then was in his mid-forties, got his twenty-three-year-old girlfriend pregnant, he turned to me for help in persuading her that, yes, she should have an abortion. This was the hardest thing I've ever had to do. . . . It felt like the bursting of my dream of having George's child. And it marked the first time he had called on me to be his friend in a way that was no longer erotic. But I acceded to George's wishes. His girlfriend had the abortion and they broke up a year later.

Today I live in New York full-time. I'm glad I had the experience of being with George. But I regard our breakup as ultimately liberating for our relationship. He's a great friend. He still takes care of me. His present to me for my fortieth birthday was a washing machine.

Even with all the unusual twists and turns our relationship took, all the heartache I endured, I have no regrets. Some people love and their hearts shrink. They get jealous and scared. Through loving George and fully embracing his idiosyncratic spirit, my heart expanded.

George Says

I seem destined to be a serial monogamist. I enjoy the intimacy and closeness one experiences by knowing someone inside out. But I don't want children. Nor do I enjoy being drawn into a girl-friend's bad mood or to be forced to deal with her idiosyncratic habits. That's why I've never lived with anyone. Yet I consider myself *very* lucky in love: I've had eight significant relationships in my life. Sloan was number four or five.

We were both outspoken and free on a personal level, yet directed in our artwork—complete anomalies to our families. I grew up a child of privilege. I was a Boy Scout, student council president, and premed student. By luck, I didn't get into medical school so visited France for a year. That's where I began a vocation as an avant-garde artist that has continued my whole life. Being an artist has and will always be more important to me than being with someone . . . even someone as special as Sloan.

I consider Sloan one of the few people on earth genuinely capable of unconditional loving. This is both a good and bad trait. She continued to love me even though I rejected her shortly after we met. I'm attracted to women who are adventurous: They'll do silly things like jump into ice-cold water or skydive. Sloan isn't fun that way, which was a bit of a sore point in the relationship for me. But not enough to keep me from wanting to be with her—most of the time.

We were monogamous—most of the time. A month after we met, I realized I'd left something at her place, so I stopped back up. I spied a pair of male shoes sticking out from under her bed. Sloan felt absolutely awful. I'd tease her about it periodically over the next few years.

During the first four years of our relationship we were like rabbits. Luckily we had the same amount of desire toward the other. But once the "rabbity" stuff stops, my nature is to start looking around. This resulted in intermittent affairs. The more I sensed Sloan was unhappy about my wandering the more I felt myself drawn toward other women.

Yet Sloan is the only partner with whom I allowed myself to entertain the notion of having a child. As I said, fatherhood wasn't something I wanted, but for a brief window I wasn't totally averse to it happening. We tried and it didn't work out. But we didn't *over-try*.

When a couple marries, so much junk gets in the way that they reach the point where there is 15 to 20 percent negativity between them. Couples who don't live together develop much less negativity. They do all the fun things—camping, traveling, movies, running, eating out . . . At the end of the day they go to their homes and don't have to deal with the other person's crap.

However, I'm a big believer that things run their course. Couples are in love for a certain amount of time. Interests wane, people change. I must constantly be stimulated, constantly evolve, or I get bored. When something stops, there's a void. But that's okay. Growing up I spent a lot of time by myself making things in Dad's workshop. This self-containment led me to be able to "self-entertain," to take care of my own needs. I don't look to external solutions to not being internally happy. I make no attempt to control other's lives, just as they should make no attempt to control mine.

When Sloan fell for one of my close friends, I wasn't terribly bothered. Since I loved both of them as human beings, it made sense that they came to love one another. Besides, I'm always becoming involved with other people.

The relationship with Sloan ultimately disintegrated because being faced with her unhappiness made me unhappy. A woman came along who was happier and younger. . . . Sloan of course was loving enough to help my new girlfriend out when she got pregnant with my child.

Although Sloan lives in New York now, I'll always consider her part of my family. She taught me to express my feelings better by forcing me to talk about what was in my heart rather than retreating into a shell.

I'm at the tail end of my eighth serious relationship. My girlfriend, who is thirty-five, wants to have a baby. I'm fifty-one now and there are no diapers in my future. The breakup will be painful, but happenstances that most people think are negative are actually vectors that push you into a new direction.

While I cherish my memories of past loves I am excited by the possibilities of future ones.

Sherry Says

If you gaze into a lover's eyes and see reflected his/her own image, beware. You are in love with someone who is totally and completely in love—unfortunately not with you.

Where Sloan Erred

It's great to accept your lover, warts and all, but sometimes love should have a *few* conditions. Although she wasn't a victim, Sloan was too understanding of George's limitations as a life partner. Thus he had no inducement to make an effort to change his self-absorbed ways. Ten years seems about eight and a-half years too long to give to a man whose narcissistic worldview prohibits him from being able to make concrete dinner plans with mutual friends.

Even after the breakup, Sloan allowed George to take advantage of her too-good nature. Perhaps that too-good nature stemmed in part from Sloan subconsciously not feeling worthy of making demands of people in her life. Perhaps not. In any case how bizarre and sad it is that she put herself through the ordeal of counseling her pregnant successor on the "pluses" of whether or not to have an abortion.

Where Sloan Shone

Sloan is emotionally generous, warm, nonpossessive and non-judgmental. She is not one to saddle lovers with unrealistic expectations. Nor is she saddled by the harboring of conventional notions of what a relationship should and shouldn't be. Just because a man doesn't proffer to her the ring, an abode peopled with a passel of kiddies, or offer complete fidelity doesn't mean she can't appreciate the positives he does offer. Sloan is also supremely capable of carrying on a professional as well as personal partnership with the one she loves.

As the years passed and Sloan began wanting more out of a partner than someone who provided excitement, fun, and creative sparks, she became able to move forward . . . alone. However, she realized that the rewards of life come through fully embracing the bitter along with the sweet. *Even with all the unusual twists and turns our relationship took, all the heartache I endured, I have no regrets.*

Where George Erred

George is a fair-weather lover. When things are good, passionate, the opposite of routine, he is content. However, should his partner make a demand or express dissatisfaction, he's not the type to make compromises. His inability to realize the audacious insensitivity he displayed toward Sloan postbreakup makes him the poster child of self-absorbed people everywhere.

Where George Shone

George suffers no crisis of self-identity or self-worth. First and foremost an artist, this self-contained man does not need a woman around to be complete. Though as he ages the joys of living alone might begin to pale.

The eight serious partners in his life would probably agree that George is great boyfriend material. He is capable of showing someone a fun time, as well as of helping her develop confidence in her inherent talents. Better yet, he is probably one of the least jealous and/or clingy men on earth. Juxtaposed alongside his need not be tied down is an ability to engage in long-term relationships. Just don't say the "f" word around him. I mean *forever*, natch.

Your Love Lesson From This Couple's Breakup

This couple was brought together by their twin idiosyncratic natures. Neither could be accused of fostering a traditional outlook. What ultimately did them in (at least in the romantic sense) was George's inability to deeply care about the needs of anyone other than "his truly."

My Biggest Heartbreak and What It Taught Me About Love

Dayton Fandray, 48, writer/musician

I picked Claudia up at a Manhattan club in the late '70s. I was wildly attracted to her as I was to anything female in those days. I was in my twenties, newly divorced, and living in a bombed-out apartment in the East Village. I took her home that night.

She showed up at the club again and we wound up having a relationship. It was never steady in the sense of regularly seeing each other. Claudia was kind of wild, which scared me. I took her to a Christmas party where she got drunk and threw drinks at people. She threw up the whole way home on the bus.

Yet, there was something about her that kept me coming back although there was often a one- or two-month gap between our get-togethers. One of those gaps lasted nine months. Then she called me or maybe it was the other way around, and we returned to our weird, irregular pattern. I thought we'd always find our way back to each other.

The last time I saw Claudia was the morning of September 20, 1981. It was the night after a Simon and Garfunkel concert in Central Park. I loaned Claudia Sinclair Lewis's *Dodsworth*. My last image of this woman was of her back heading south on First Avenue, carrying one of my all-time favorite books.

I moved to Los Angeles and again lost touch with my sometime lover. By the time I tried to find her a few years later she'd moved on—no forwarding address.

Fifteen years later I moved back to New York and on a beautiful fall evening, stood in Central Park and said, "Damn, I screwed up."

I have been in love so few times that I just didn't allow myself to recognize what I felt for Claudia until it was too late. Now I realize that whenever someone walks out your door, it may be the last time you see her. So you shouldn't let her go just *assuming* things will come together. You've got to *talk* to each other.

It's appropriate that I gave Claudia *Dodsworth* since the premise of the book is lost love. I wonder if she still has it. I hope she looks at it from time to time and thinks about me.

Tom & Diana

Relationship b: 1985; d:1996

Chapter 19

Ignorance Isn't Bliss

Tom Says

I've spent my life trying to do the right thing. My father expected me to accomplish certain tasks—graduate from college, get married, buy a house, have children. And God help me if I didn't complete those things in the proper order.

I always knew I was gay—in seventh grade I chose a gym locker that gave me a great view of the coach changing his clothes. Given my familial expectations, it was obvious that while I was inherently honest, I'd have to accept lying as part of my lifestyle.

It's not that I didn't enjoy sex with women—I started sleeping with girls in the ninth grade. But it wasn't what I craved. I went to my first gay bar when I was a freshman at college, not long before I met my future wife. Diana didn't have the prettiest face on the block but she had a dynamite body. And we both liked to party.

That's something we still have in common. To this day we can sit together in a bar and have a great time.

No, I wasn't deeply attracted to her but I needed a wife to cover up my homosexuality. I had something Diana lacked in her life and really wanted—to be part of an intact family. My parents and I loved showing her a good time. And because her parents were lower-middle-class it wasn't a hardship for Diana, who'd grown up poor, to be around a well-to-do clan.

During our courtship I'd drop her off after a date and head to a gay bar. Two months before Diana and I got engaged I met up with an old girlfriend. We had sex on the living room floor of her sorority house.

Essentially I married Diana because I could pull the wool over her eyes. The truth was and always will be that I'm very attracted to men. After we tied the knot I stopped sleeping with other women.

I wasn't unhappy being married. Diana was my best friend. She would tell her friends I was the best husband in the world. I'd notice when she got a new haircut; help her pick out flattering clothes . . . I was supportive when she talked about her problems. On the outside things were great. I was a director of youth at our church. I worked for a state senator. But whenever I traveled on business I'd find a gay bar so fast your head would spin.

Having children was the best part of the marriage and the part that ultimately drove us apart. I remember looking at my second child and thinking, "How can I expect my daughter to be honest with me if I'm living a lie each and every day?" For the first time I started to feel—not guilty, that's a pretty big word, but like the walls were starting to close in. I was lonely.

Diana says she never suspected I was gay but she had a great ability to deny what she knew. For instance, she'd regularly find folded up pieces of paper in my pockets with men's names and phone numbers on them. I wanted to tell her but I was afraid that if I confessed I was gay she wouldn't be my best friend anymore. I mean if someone asks, "Do these pants make me look fat?" you don't say, "They make your thighs look elephantine." I guess I also had a great ability to deny.

In the fall of 1994 I went to Washington on business and met a handsome gay man who was open about his sexual orientation, yet very successful in business. I'd assumed if I ever came out it would be the death knell to my career. Ted and I started seeing each other every chance we got. While Diana thought I was "interviewing" I'd be shacking up with Ted in San Francisco, Denver, Washington.

I was very disenchanted with working so hard and tired of pretending to be straight. I started picking fights with Diana—not to get her to leave me, but to change the situation. I told her I'd been seeing someone, a man, but was ending it. She said, "Don't end it. There's someone at work I like. I'm gonna go to a movie with him." That was the beginning of the end of our marriage.

I had always tried not to make my dating public, and here she was flaunting her new affair. I did end my relationship and even continued sleeping with Diana. But she started behaving horribly—going to work and not coming home until the next morning. Our children were three and one and a half. I believe Diana acted so reprehensibly because she needed a lover's reassurance that she was a beautiful woman. Joe kept telling her, "You deserve better than Tom." He was a major influence in convincing her to pack the kids up and leave.

I was willing to stay married if she'd stop seeing Joe. She wanted to stay married and continue seeing him. It was an ugly six months. She had a sheriff issue a restraining order and kick me out of the house. She claims I tried to turn the power off but the power company has records proving they told her it wasn't going to be shut off. I *did* threaten to have her arrested if she took the kids out of state to attend her sister's wedding.

There was lots of name-calling and lots of fights. Our friends were caught in the middle. If only we'd calmly sat down and figured things out instead of listening to everyone else tell us what we should do. . . . My children saw and heard things they had no need to witness. The only winners were the lawyers. We ended up having to file for bankruptcy, and the divorce decree gave Diana less than the amount of my initial offer to her.

Through it all I missed my best friend. Once she left Joe everything became okay again. Diana likes my current partner; I like hers. Diana jets around the world with her pilot boyfriend; I'm the chairman of the PTA. My friends ask, "How could Diana possibly have let you take custody of the kids?" Well, she doesn't contribute to them financially. I don't say anything negative to the girls about their mother. I don't say anything positive either—just stuff like, "Mommy called today. You should call her back."

My relationship with Barry is much fuller than what I shared with Diana. There are no secrets or shadows. You couldn't possibly look at my family and think what we share is bad. Even my parents accept my homosexuality and have come to love my lover.

I won't apologize for having been married. I tried to be the best husband I could be. And I'm so fortunate to have biological children. Do I have any regrets? No, outside of the horrible divorce period when we behaved so badly. To me, regrets are opportunities lost, and I certainly never lost an opportunity.

It's a great feeling to be who I am today versus whom I was ten years ago. There are no how-to manuals outlining how to be a gay guy in a heterosexual marriage.

Diana Says

Although my parents divorced when I was in the third grade, I was raised to follow a traditional lifestyle. The plan was for me to go away to college, meet a boy, marry, have kids, a white picket fence, and live happily ever after. It wasn't in my grand scheme to marry a man who'd ultimately leave me because he was gay.

I've always been attracted to athletes. The first thing I noticed about Tom when we met at college was his great swimmer's body. We lived in the same dorm and hung out a lot together and I soon noticed other things about him: He enjoyed being the center of attention and was a master at convincing people to do things they didn't really want to do. We began dating each other but it wasn't exclusive. I didn't know we were seriously involved until Tom convinced me that getting married would be a great thing. He said we'd have a fabulous life together. Did I say how good he was at swaying others to his point of view? Anyway, we got engaged and started living together.

Tom was my best friend and our sex life was good. Well, we had sex a lot. Once in a while a guy would call and ask to speak to my fiancé. I asked Tom what that was about. He confessed that he used to experiment with men, but had come to realize he preferred women. I had no reason to disbelieve him, so seventeen days into my twenty-third year I walked down the aisle.

Our wedding night was fun. We spent the honeymoon driving from Michigan to Iowa where we were going to live. Looking back, I'd have to say that our marriage was one of friendship and sex—but not passion. Tom was romantic—sending flowers, coming home from the grocery store with bubble bath for me. But passion—I discovered what that was much later on.

Tom was attending grad school during the day. At night he worked at a bar. Sometimes he wouldn't get home until 2 A.M. I'd leave for work at 8 A.M. (I sold cosmetics), so do the math on how much time we spent together. Two or three times I found a copy of *Playgirl* hidden in Tom's things. He told me he looked at the naked guys' pictures for inspiration when he worked out. I was like, "right, whatever." I wanted to believe him so I did. As far as

I was concerned, I had a straight, faithful husband and a marriage that would last forever.

A few years in, we bought a house. Having kids seemed like the logical next step so I got pregnant. Life was good. Then Tom, who's a lobbyist, announced he was moving us to Washington, D.C., where he had a job interview. His first brilliant idea: I should rent a U-Haul and drive our two babies in diapers cross-country. He'd fly down separately. His second brilliant idea: The children and I would be exiled to the Washington suburbs while he lived in town Monday through Friday and commuted "home" on weekends. When I objected to this plan by telling him I didn't want to essentially become a single mom, he accused me of not being supportive. For once I stood firm. We'd move *when* he got a job and I wouldn't be shunted to the hinterlands. He started traveling a lot on interviews and coming home with elaborate, entertaining stories about his potential bosses and co-workers.

I fell for all of it until I was forcibly ripped from my cocoon. Tom came home from a long weekend away and announced he couldn't stand lying anymore. He hadn't been kibitzing with politicians but in Denver skiing with his boyfriend. I laughed. It seemed so outlandish. Tom insisted he was telling the truth. He admitted that for the past few months he'd been sneaking away for little vacations with this man who—yes!—lived in Washington, D.C.

Although Tom said he'd never done anything that had jeopardized my health, I insisted we have AIDS tests. We continued living in the same house, even sharing the same bed. Occasionally we'd have sex. I wanted to keep the marriage together. I thought, "My parents got divorced. The cycle of failure had to end."

I started confiding my problems to Joe, this guy at work. He took advantage of my vulnerability and we started seeing each other. Although Tom and I had agreed to turn our marriage into an open one, he got jealous of my boyfriend. The second I got

home from a date he'd start drilling me. *Why had I been out so late?*
What had I done? If he'd been drinking, his verbal abuse would be
worse. If I wouldn't answer his questions he'd push me. Once he
did it so hard that I fell down.

Tom confessed the real facts of his life in April; I left him the following September. He came home drunk one night too many, so I
packed up the girls and we checked into a motel under assumed
names. Tom continued an abusive campaign. I wouldn't take his
phone calls at work so he'd fax me ten to twenty letters a day. In
order to move back into the house I had to sign a restraining order
kicking him off the premises and barring him from coming back
and harassing us. He'd then send letters threatening to stop paying the electricity bills.

Because he was the one with the larger income he wound up
getting the house and the girls and I moved into an apartment. I
was very bitter but he had the better attorney. In our state judges
rarely award alimony so I didn't bother asking for it. I got a job as
a mortgage broker.

Things between us stayed ugly for close to two years. Even at
the height of our feud Tom and I would occasionally watch a ball
game together at a local bar, or go together to a school function.
Joe gave me grief for hanging out with my husband. Finally I
broke up with Joe.

Tom and I had joint custody of the girls. Things settled into a
pattern and Tom and I both settled into new relationships. I moved
in with Bob, an airline pilot, while Tom fell in love with a teacher
named Barry. At first it was uncomfortable seeing the two guys displaying affection for each other—it still is, but I'm used to it.

Tom got an opportunity to work in London for a year and
asked if he could take the girls. He went on about what a fabulous
experience it would be for them to live in a foreign country, and
swore he'd bring them back to Iowa.

He swayed me as usual and the four of them took off on their exciting adventure. Only when the gig was over Tom, Barry, and the girls moved to Washington. I could have taken Tom back to court but we'd agreed not to fight over the girls anymore. I don't want to ask them to choose between their father and mother. Plus, he is a much better parent than I am—more patient and more active in school activities. I know the girls love their life but I wonder sometimes if Tom works on them—saying stuff like, "Oh, if you lived with your mom you wouldn't have your friends in Washington."

I don't let his manipulations upset me anymore. He did it to me at age twenty-two and when we were divorcing. It's Tom being Tom. Besides, I see the girls as often as I want. I fly to Washington and stay at Tom and Barry's.

If Tom hadn't lied to me about his sexuality I wouldn't have married him. Yet, I don't regret our ten years together. I have the girls and Tom is one of my closest friends. And he'll have to live with the knowledge of his deception for the rest of his life.

I had my head in the sand during the marriage. All I saw was the white picket fence, two cars, frequent vacations, and a husband that cared for me. Tom made a big deal about my birthdays. He loved to go shopping with me. That seemed like enough. My present relationship is so much more fulfilling, passionate, and fun. Bob cares completely about my feelings. If I didn't want to drive across the country alone in a U-Haul, he'd understand.

I hope my girls learn from their mother's mistakes—don't get married just to get married, don't get swept up in someone else's fantasy, don't ignore the truth because it's easier to live a lie. Tom cheated during the entire marriage and I had no clue. I suspected he masturbated while he looked at *Playgirl*, but I never dreamt he was going to gay bars.

If Tom had left me for another woman, I could have tried to fix the problem. *Well, she does that for him; I can, too.* But the way things were—I didn't have the right equipment to fight for my husband.

When you marry at twenty-three, you look to your partner to help define you. Now I define myself and if Tom or Bob don't like who I am, it's their problem.

Punch/Counterpunch

DIANA: He has to live with what he did for the rest of his life.
TOM: I have no trouble sleeping at night.

DIANA: Tom manipulated his way into getting everything he wants.
TOM: As if manipulation is a bad word!

TOM: During the conversation when I confessed I was gay, I remember a whole lot of laughter as opposed to sadness.
DIANA: It was a nervous laugh. Kind of like, "This really can't be true!" I didn't want to believe him so I laughed and he was able to delude himself into thinking he hadn't just detonated my life.

Sherry Says

The only love match that doesn't possess some inherent incompatibilities is one between a narcissist and his/her favorite person. For pairings that actually involve a *pair*, differences between them needn't be definitive harbingers of doom. One might be a night owl while the other is a zealous proponent of the "early to bed, early to rise" dictum. Or perhaps one regularly chomps down venison while the other is vegan. Or one half of this terribly-in-love twosome lives in L.A. while the other is a diehard East Coaster. Or a Muslim and Moonie meet, meld hearts and bodies, but when it comes to religious beliefs—whoa, baby!

Every couple eventually faces a make-or-break issue, most of which can be resolved with an unswerving commitment to working things out. However, Diana and Tom had a double hurdle to scale: Not only was he a "man-izer" but a master liar as well. And Diana's willingness (eagerness) to be a dupe put her in the running for Grand Prizewinner in the Victim of Love sweepstakes.

Where Tom Erred

He erred by lying to the person who loved and trusted him more than anyone else in the world. *Essentially I married Diana because I could pull the wool over her eyes.* While I empathize with his pain at having to hide his true sexual nature from the world, it doesn't excuse his deceit. Although Diana says she wouldn't have married him if she'd known Tom was gay, I'm not so sure. Despite his preference for men, Tom and his wife shared an active sex life and caring camaraderie. And Diana did love being parented by Tom's parents.

For a guy who has spent his life trying to do the right thing— Tom has committed more than his share of fouls.

Where Tom Shone

He's a good father. Hopefully he is teaching his children to be proud of who they are and never to marry someone essentially because they can pull the wool over their partner's eyes.

Where Diana Erred

She who refuses to see can't complain (much) about being blindsided. Diana's desperate desire to lead a "traditional" lifestyle led her to ignore the many, many warning signs that she was not in Ozzie and Harriet Land.

In her defense, she was young and malleable when Tom "manipulated" her into marriage. However, as some of the best years of her life trickled away, her head remained tucked under quicksand. *I wanted to believe in him, so I did. As far as I was concerned, I had a straight, faithful husband and a marriage that would last forever.*

Her white-picket-fence dreamworld was really a house of cards destined to collapse with one hearty blow. But Diana held her breath, held her tongue, and passively co-conspired to remain locked into a marriage that was sour at its core.

When the cocoon was ripped open, and her heart and ego received huge boo-boos, Diana's judgment became impaired, leading her to make precipitous and disastrous decisions. I call your attention to lobbying for an open marriage, falling under the sway of yet another manipulative man; and not hiring a divorce lawyer sharp enough to win his client a settlement that should befit a wife who was screwed-over by her husband screwing another man. It's also a concern that she allowed Tom to take the kids away because she'd previously agreed not to fight with her ex over custody issues. A woman who looks for wisdom on how to run her life everywhere but inside herself, needs to wise up fast.

Where Diana Shone

She's a survivor. A lesser woman, upon discovering that her husband of a decade preferred men (and always had!) might crawl under the covers and never emerge. Divorce is never easy and often ugly, but Diana eventually reemerged from the embers scorched, yet standing.

Extra points are awarded to her for not turning bitter. Tom's betrayal left her (hopefully) more cautious about men but willing to love and trust again. And she's able to maintain a friendship with her ex, not just for the good of the children, but because while finally hip to his con artist ways, she still values his presence in her life.

Your Love Lesson From This Couple's Breakup

For years Diana lived in a bubble. Her subconscious philosophy was: *See no evil, hear no evil, speak no evil.* She longed so badly to live in the beautiful, sanitized white-picket-fence world revered by her parents that she chose to live a lie rather than pierce the bubble and voice what she knew in her heart: The father of her children lusted after *Playgirl*'s pinups of the month. However, once the truth was out (outed) life was chaotic and painful but ultimately richer.

It's always better to accept and deal with what life hands you rather than to hide from the unpleasant reality. Listen to your gut instinct. It's your inner compass and will never steer you wrong.

Marguerite & Tom

Relationship b: 1993; d: 1999

Chapter 20

Without Mutual Yuks, Life Together Is Yuck

Marguerite Says

I'm furious with Tom for wasting the prime birthing years of my life. I was with him from ages twenty-four through thirty. Tom is eighteen years older than I am and there was so much of a divide between us that sometimes it felt like I was sleeping with a friend of my parents.

We met at the Arthur Murray Dance Studios. We were part of a clique who hung out several nights a week doing the tango, polka, and every other ballroom dance under the sun. Tom seemed so smart and quick-witted and mature that I lost my personality around him—he made me *that* uncomfortable.

I was guarded around males. I didn't have a strong bond with my dad and—this part is awful—I was raped when I was nineteen. In college I was an antisocial nerd with a math degree so the men didn't come running.

For a long time Tom and I were platonic friends. We did lots of fun stuff together—-even went on little trips—and he never made a sexual move. That helped me relax around him.

Two years after we met Tom and I went away for the weekend. We were lying in bed Saturday morning and he asked, "Marguerite, are we just platonic or is there something more here?"

He'd never called me beautiful, or even kissed me so it seemed weird when he asked that question. When he finally made a move, I was hesitant but receptive.

Though Tom wasn't my first lover, he was the first person who helped me deal with my anger against men. He was patient and sweet. When it came to my career, he became my cheerleader. I worked in retail and hated it. We heard a radio commercial for a broadcasting course and, as Tom put it, he watched a lightbulb go off in my head. He encouraged me to enroll in the school though he wasn't so happy later when I got a great DJ job that had me working weekends.

While my life was changing, Tom's was stagnant. He was a lawyer but had a half-assed job that didn't pay much money so he moved back into his childhood home with his elderly, ailing parents.

The next three years, our relationship was pretty intact. We weren't talking marriage but saw each other everyday and had a good sex life. Things changed after Tom's parents died and I moved into his house.

Tom's friends blame our breakup on my not liking the house. I'm not that shallow. But this was an old people's house. These particular old people had been pack rats. There were baby carriages from 1952, a freestanding cabinet filled with southern New England telephone bills circa the 1940s, linoleum and wallpaper from 1966. There was no counter space in the kitchen and if you lifted something up, there'd be a bug under it! This was seriously disgusting, not to mention very bad *feng shui*.

Tom didn't make room for my things when I moved in. Yet he had drawers full of his dead mother's underwear! When I protested he said, "I didn't expect you to bring stuff with you." He finally shifted things around, but *very* grudgingly.

He was also grudging on the financial level. During all our dating years we'd gone Dutch. Now I was at a rough point in my career transition and I needed him to support me. It started kicking in that he wasn't making room for me in his house, in his wallet, and I didn't hear him making plans to marry me any time soon. When I'd talk about us someday having kids, he would freak!

I was twenty-nine. Although Tom's friends were in their fifties I was a good sport about hanging out with them. Once I brought Tom to a party my friend was throwing. It was the most freezing night of the year and Tom picked a fight and drove off, leaving me without a ride. He finally came back an hour and a half later.

I started developing a circle of friends my own age. I joined the Junior League and took comedy improv classes. I had to find somewhere to put my energy because around the fourth year Tom and I were together, our sex life died. During a one-year period we had sex maybe twelve times. I wasn't afraid of men anymore; I felt flirtatious and ready to experiment sexually. Tom's method of making love was this: I stood naked in front of him, he'd cop a feel of my bosom, I'd lie down, he'd get on top of me— no foreplay, in and out, over and done. If I suggested trying something different, he accused me of needing to be in control. I bought videotapes made by a sex therapist. We tried a shrink. This helped, but just for a little while.

Easter 1999 we reached the point of no return. I'd been working on the relationship for five months. I had literally stopped hanging out with my younger friends to stay home with Tom.

Then came that fateful Easter or as I later referred to it: The Day of the Salad Bowls Fight. Although I didn't cook a lot, I set out to make an amazing holiday meal for twenty-five of Tom's relatives. I cooked leg of lamb, garlic mashed potatoes, orange and ginger soup. There was just a little mesclun salad so I didn't feel we needed the bowls Tom had taken out. Tom always liked things done in a certain way. But I'd figured out how to work him to get my way. I said, "It was so sweet of you to do all the shopping yesterday and to set the table but I've given this meal a lot of thought and I don't think we need the salad bowls."

He hit the ceiling, screaming that I wanted to control him. He said, "For forty-four years my family has eaten salad out of bowls and that's what we're gonna continue doing." Then out it came. He said, "I don't want to marry you. I never did want to marry you and I never will."

I hadn't brought the subject up for a year. I said, "Let's not do this now. We have to get it together for your family."

His relatives showed up a half hour early. The meal went fine. Later, when Tom and I were washing the dishes, I was on a high. I thought we'd gotten through this horrible fight. He said, "You're no fun. I want someone fun in my life."

That crushed me. I'm *a lot* of fun. Tom repeated that he'd never marry me and I knew it was over. We didn't talk about it but clearly we were history.

I didn't have the guts to move out but over the next months I started taking lots of classes and hanging out with my friends. At a party I clicked with a guy my age and I knew it was time.

In July I threw a huge surprise fiftieth birthday party for Tom. He was very touched. The next day I started looking for apartments. I quickly found one and dropped the bomb.

He looked as shaken as the day his mother had died but he never asked me to stay.

The day I moved out I felt on top of the world. I didn't really mourn Tom 'cause I'd done most of my mourning while we were under the same roof. I fell directly into a rebound relationship with the guy I'd met at that party. That didn't work out and I moved on.

Looking back, what I had with Tom was Relationship 101. I got my BA, masters, and Ph.D., then graduated.

Tom is a wonderful person and was a great mentor to me. But at this stage of my life I don't want a teacher, but a partner. The age difference broke us up. We're in different life phases. I'm in my "go go" years—I've got energy and drive to burn. Tom doesn't have any more goals and he hates change.

When I tell new friends about my failed relationship, they say, "He was eighteen years older than you, had never been in a serious relationship, and lived with his parents?!" As if to say, "What were you thinking?" I rebut with, "But he's such a nice person."

And he is. He's also articulate and brilliant and handsome and he strengthened me to the point where I didn't need him anymore.

Tom Says

Marguerite is the first woman I ever lived with. But she wasn't the first woman in my life. I had two important love affairs in my twenties, then no women for around eight years. Subsequently I dated someone for a short time, followed by another long dry spell, then a relationship I hoped would lead to a marriage as solid as the one between my parents. It didn't. My lifestyle isn't one that attracts women. I don't work for a big corporation or make a lot of money.

What brought Marguerite and me together was a love of dancing. We were the youngest members of our group at Arthur Murray. The other dancers were in their mid to late sixties.

When Marguerite first learned that I was seventeen years her senior, the blood literally drained from her face. Yet she asked me to escort her to a swing dance evening at a club. We had drinks afterward and she said, "When I'm your age, you'll be sixty-two." The discomfort was palpable. But she kept asking me out. Each time I'd think, Okay, she'll either say, "I really like you but we should just be friends" or "Why don't you give me a kiss?"

Instead, she continued driving me crazy with mixed signals. One minute she'd be holding my hand, the next trying to set me up with an older female friend. After a movie date I gave her a *serious* kiss. We never talked about it. If I'd been younger I would have seduced her and it would probably have broken us up. Having suffered a sexual assault, she needed things to be her way. And we did so many interesting activities together that it *almost* made up for the lack of sex.

On our weekend away it was killing me being in bed with her. I'd had it: It was either move ahead or end the torment. So I spoke up. And we made love so passionately it was fuel-injected!

The relationship was really great for a while. I enjoyed watching Marguerite go from math major to radio DJ. My own situation had tanked. I'd left a fairly decent job to move back home to help out my aging parents. Incidentally Marguerite was more comfortable around my parents than any other woman I'd ever met.

The moment we moved in together our relationship started to peter out. I was in the midst of preparing for a nerve-wracking trial. Marguerite immediately wanted me to prepare a room for her things. I said, "Let me try this case and in two weeks I'll do whatever you need." We had a really nasty fight. She went *nuts*. I thought, What kind of animal can't realize that I'm distracted right now by external pressures? That was the first time I questioned whether Marguerite was the woman I wanted to marry.

She had underlying frustrations about what she saw as my lack of ambition. My greatest accomplishments had already happened. Other aspects of the relationship that went wrong are harder to define. She's very willful. I am, too, but I'm better at compromising and she needs to learn a little temperance.

Our sex life went south. From the beginning, Marguerite needed a patient, sensitive style of lovemaking that was unique to my experience. All the other women I'd been with loved me making love to them. Marguerite made me feel inadequate. I'm not a slam, bam, thank you ma'am kind of guy. Nor do I feel like every time we make love it has to last for hours!

I said to Marguerite, "Your criticisms about my sexual insensitivity make me feel like a lab rat that learns after two or three tries not to touch the lever that's gonna shock him. This has to be fun for me, too."

It got to the point where I didn't want to have sex. So Marguerite bought these love videos. I never liked porn and I didn't find these tapes entertaining in the least. Plus I wasn't going to learn anything. I knew how to make love. But I acted like I thought the tapes were cool.

I found the therapist visit intriguing. She said, "What's up with you?" I answered, "We don't have a sex life." The therapist said, "It's a power struggle." I thought she was right but Marguerite and I never talked about it afterward. The therapist said we didn't need any more sessions.

Marguerite was frustrated that I didn't propose or want children. I felt the tension had to be worked out of the relationship before I could make that kind of commitment.

I put up with a lot of Marguerite's stuff because I valued the good qualities that come with it. I was open-minded. I listened to reasonable suggestions. But she'd micromanage my life, then call *me* controlling! I said, "Don't tell me how to pay my bills. The relationship worked better when you looked up to me. Now you think you know it all."

She never learned how to bide her time. She had no patience. In the middle of a silly fight about salad bowls she provoked a discussion about whether or not I'd marry her. After my family came and went, Marguerite and I were just starting to relax and she asked again, "Are we gonna get married one day?"

I said, "Let me get a good night's sleep and we'll talk about it at a neutral moment."

The truth is I wanted to be married as much as she did. I never said, "Hey, Marguerite, I'm a lot older and I have less time for having children." I felt we should consider whether if we did become a family unit we'd love jumping in the car and doing things together, or would Mommy and Daddy always be unhappy and angry. Marguerite didn't have the maturity to think that far ahead. How could she? She was barely thirty.

I was willing to wait a long, long time for the conditions to be right for us to marry but I understood why she moved out. The day she left I thought I was going to have a heart attack. I was short of breath and so anguished that I'd never asked her to marry me.

If I had a second chance I'd sell the house so we could start somewhere fresh. But it still wouldn't work if every time we made love, I felt like a lab rat about to be hit by electric shocks.

Sherry Says

This breakup story does not have a culprit. The ballad of Marguerite and Tom is not "Hey Won't You Play Another Somebody Done Somebody Wrong Song?" but "You Don't Send Me Flowers Anymore."

This couple became so wrapped up in their individual agendas and needs that they forgot one of the principal commandments of building a solid relationship: Thou Shalt Have Fun Together.

Marguerite and Tom went from dancing cheek to cheek to dancing around each other. Each became so determined not to lose ground to the other (metaphorically and literally) that they started battling for power instead of striving toward unity. With all the fighting, silences that were worth one thousand angry words, and mutual avoidance that came to fill their waking hours, they drained the relationship of positive energy. Eventually these listless lovers simply ran out of steam.

Where Marguerite Erred

Her initial modus operandi in this May/October romance was an unapologetic self-absorption. She took Tom's tendering of friendship, guidance, and patience without considering the psychological cost of his largesse. Offering to fix up a man who's nuts about you with another woman is not an act of kindness.

In her heart of hearts Marguerite always felt this was her starter relationship; that ultimately she'd want to be with someone closer to her age. Yet she played things out to the bitter end—complaining that Tom was wasting her prime birthing years rather than realizing that his biological clock was ticking away at a much swifter pace.

Once they became cohabiting lovers her modus operandi was (unapologetic) manipulation. *I figured out how to work him to get my way.* How much less vitriolic the climate between them might have become if Marguerite hadn't assumed she knew Tom's thoughts, beliefs, and goals, but actually tried to penetrate his defensive layers and gotten to the heart of the man. But the walls guarding *her* heart were so thick that she took every slight from Tom (e.g., his not instantly making room in his house for her stuff) as further proof of his intractability. He was an ungiving, selfish man and that was that. End of story.

On the sexual front Marguerite was certainly right to request sensitivity from her lover. Too bad it didn't occur to her to make her request in a sensitive manner.

Where Marguerite Shone

She worked hard to take back her sexuality and not to distrust all men in the wake of the rape. She also had a big, big heart and generous spirit as evidenced by her throwing her estranged lover an elaborate surprise birthday party. Okay, there was some guilt involved here as she was about to drop the "I'm leaving" bomb.

In the early stages of the relationship she was able to accept Tom's suggestions on how to better her life. As she came into her own it's admirable that she wanted to help him evolve, too. However, this was tempered by the fact that she wanted him to evolve into the person *she* wanted him to be.

Where Tom Erred

He characterized the relationship between his parents as solid. However, there were likely some slippery goings-on as well which might help account for Tom's reaching his mid-forties without ever having lived with a woman other than mama.

Tom's generally passive attitude (*My greatest accomplishments had already happened*) extends itself to the relationship arena. Consider that he waited two years before asking the woman who haunted his dreams if she was interested in him as more than a friend.

He wanted Marguerite to grow as a person, but was subsequently threatened when the chickie grew capable of flying unaided from the nest. *This relationship worked better when you looked up to me.*

Tom accused Marguerite of sending mixed signals during their courtship. He committed the selfsame "sin" once the relationship turned serious: asking her to move in, then not making her feel welcome. Fine, don't immediately empty out your dead mother's underwear drawer but at least buy a bottle of champagne to mark your longtime girlfriend's change of address!

He found it easy to blow up at Marguerite, but agonizingly difficult to admit to her the root of his frustrations. He thought the shrink visit was enlightening but didn't let Marguerite in on his emotional discoveries. And, why oh why, didn't he ever tell Marguerite that yes, he did eventually want to marry her, did eventually want her to be the mother of his children? His passivity and fear led him to postpone proposing until things seemed *perfect*. While he's correct that marriage isn't the answer to a troubled relationship, at some point if the love and will are there you have to hold your nose and dive in without being fully cognizant of the depth of the pool.

Where Tom Shone

He's a sensitive, patient, loving man who could truly empathize with the pain and trauma Marguerite suffered as a result of her sexual assault. Kudos to a kindhearted guy.

Your Love Lesson From This Couple's Breakup

There isn't much these two agree on. Marguerite is sure Tom is eighteen years her senior; he says seventeen. Marguerite feels the point of no return for their relationship was The Salad Bowls Fight. To Tom, it was the day she moved in and went ballistic because he hadn't prepared a room for her stuff. A major reason for these disparate views is that somewhere along the way these two forgot how to talk to each other, or rather forgot how to *hear* what the other was saying.

This relationship might not have been built to last. Marguerite wants to be with someone who is in his "go go" years. Tom deserves a partner whose personality and lifestyle won't threaten his treasured status quo.

They became so exhausted from "working" on their problems that not only did they stop working at them, they stopped playing. And a couple who doesn't laugh together has no hope of staying together.

Chapter 21

Infidelity Needn't Be a Deal-Breaker

Jay Says

The first time I cheated on Sydney I was able to justify it in my mind. She'd been ignoring me; the temptation of this other woman throwing herself at me was just too great. The second time—well, I just screwed up.

I wasn't raised to be a cheater. I'm an only child of parents that gave me everything I needed. I had as good clothes and food as any of the twenty-two thousand people in our small town in Kansas.

Before meeting Sydney I had my share of girlfriends. I spent two years in the army, then some time in California. When I went back home this worldly twenty-five-year-old, and clapped eyes on Sydney, I instantly made inquiries about just who was this dynamite-looking gal.

Right away I liked her more than I wanted to. We were dating close to a year when she said her folks were moving to Colorado. I suggested that instead of going with them, she marry me.

Sydney and I had a big church wedding, followed by a reception at her parents' place for one hundred and fifty people. There were lights strung up, a fully stocked bar, and a barbershop quartet walking the grounds singing. That evening Sydney and I drove to Fort Worth, Texas, for our honeymoon. We consummated our relationship. I felt like a very lucky guy.

Fifteen months later our first baby came along. I traveled some for my job. I worked for the aircraft company that built the lunar spacecraft that ultimately sent a man to the moon.

After the second of our three daughters was born I took a job for a pipeline business based in Tulsa, Oklahoma. I had an expense account, company car, and access to a villa in Acapulco—one occasionally used by Liz and Dick Burton—for client entertaining. The drawback was my being gone two weeks a month out of four.

When I was home, it didn't seem to make a difference to Sydney or the girls. They didn't seem to need me for anything. But Sydney's best friend Lynn did. Lynn had been married to my best friend Dave. He was killed and Lynn was constantly in our house. Understandably she was upset and lonely. I can't recall exactly how things came about . . . guess I was in the wrong spot at the wrong time.

Looking back I believe I had an early midlife crisis. It was nice to think that a woman other than Sydney found me attractive.

Sydney discovered the affair. I left for a few months but I kept working on Sydney to take me back. Sleeping with your wife's best friend is one of those things a wife may forgive but she can't forget. We went to a marriage counselor for a few sessions. It was creepy. After our second meeting I said to Sydney, "He's a brick short of a full load. I think he's gonna cause *more* trouble between us."

A few sessions later the counselor's wife filed for divorce. Sydney agreed we could stop going to him. I still see this nut—

a sixty-year-old with a gray ponytail and ratty sweatpants—jogging around town.

Sydney and I eased back into the marriage. I had been given a second chance. But there was an undercurrent between us that didn't go away.

Still, there were plenty of good times. I traveled a lot but I'd usually make it back on Friday night to join Sydney and the girls on the twenty-eight-foot cruiser we kept out at the lake every summer weekend. And we'd take great family vacations. Our best was a one-month-long motor home trip—Sydney, the three girls, myself, and a big, brown-eyed basset hound.

Ten years after the Lynn episode, twenty years into the marriage, things were strained on both sides. There was little communication and lots of tension. We both felt ignored by the other. Even when I wasn't on the road, I wasn't home. Instead, I hung out with work buddies—drinking and partying. A lot of the guys had family problems—most brought on by themselves.

I started doing things I shouldn't, like getting messed up with some female. It was a heavy involvement. Since we lived in a small town, it was only a matter of time—three, four months—before someone told Sydney what was what. I think she already knew deep down, but nobody likes having her nose rubbed in it.

When Sydney said she knew about Linda, I broke out in a sweat. I felt guilty but also relieved. I didn't have to hide anymore. This sounds childish but I got mad at her for being mad at me. Who knows why? People do strange things at different points in their lives.

We mutually decided to split. I moved to an apartment one mile from the house so I could be close to the kids. To me, my wife was still the most attractive girl in the world and the best mother that walked the earth. Even during the worst of times I never verbally abused Sydney . . . just hurt her with some of my actions.

The night before our divorce was final, two years after the separation, we sat up talking until 1:00 in the morning. Things seemed like they'd gone too far to back out, though I'm sure with a little coaxing on both sides we would have gotten back together.

Over the next few years I saw the girls constantly. The few times I saw Sydney, we were cordial. I knew she was dating this guy for a while, and yes, it bothered me.

Throughout my adult working life expense accounts had given me access to anything I wanted. That included lots of booze. In 1985 I lost my job and decided to stop spending so many nights out with the guys drinking whiskey.

The company Sydney worked for was relocating. It was a great receptionist job but she didn't want to uproot the girls to Salt Lake City. She asked me if I wanted to move back to the house. Not back with her: I'd live on the top floor and pay Sydney rent. That way we'd be able to make the mortgage payments.

This arrangement went on for nearly a year. I dated occasionally, as did Sydney. It wasn't fun watching her go off with other men.

I got another job in the oil and gas industry. Then one of my daughters came to me and said, "Daddy, what are you doing New Year's Eve?" I said, "Honey, I haven't thought about it." She said, "Mom isn't doing anything. Would you consider taking her to dinner?" I said, "If your mom is willing, I am, too."

Sydney and I went out for dinner and dancing. We laughed and talked. After that, sometimes I'd have dinner with Sydney and the girls instead of going upstairs to my rooms.

One night I took Sydney out and said, "If God would answer my prayers, the one thing I'd ask for would be for us to get back together for the rest of our lives."

She asked for a few days to think about it. Thank God, she decided to give me a third chance.

The night before the ceremony I was taking pictures and said, "Let's have a little wedding rehearsal." Sydney's dad cracked, "Hell, we had the rehearsal twenty years ago."

We got married in our house with the balcony open and the breeze blowing. My brother-in-law, who's a minister, performed the vows.

Lots of exes try to reconcile. The same problems that tripped them up in the past reappear. For Sydney and me, it's been relatively easy. I appreciate everything *so* much more. There was always a deep love but during the first marriage we were too busy raising kids and keeping up with the Joneses to make time for each other. Now when one of us is bothered, the other *really* listens. Another thing that's different: This time around we fight instead of bottling it up.

In 1997 I had a heart transplant. A brush with death really shows you what's important. And what's important is my family.

I give advice to my kids, who are married and have blessed me with five grandchildren. I say, "Don't let problems get too deep. Get stuff handled." Then I add, "Do as I say, not as I did."

Sydney Says

Officially Jay and I divorced and remarried twice. In actuality, it feels like we've had three entirely different marriages.

My blessing was learning from experience that a couple can divorce and not hate each other forever. When I was five my parents split up but stayed friendly. Mom looked like Ava Gardner. She left Wichita and her two kids to go to New York and be a model. Dad married a woman who became the most wonderful stepmother ever.

I was a cheerleader, up for homecoming queen in junior college, had plenty of boyfriends—all that stuff. At age eighteen, I went with ten friends to a wedding reception at the American Legion. I looked across the room and saw this unbelievably handsome guy. I said, "Who is that?" and pointed. Jay's friends saw me and told him some girl was pointing at him. He looked up, said, "I've never seen her in my life," and went back to his conversation.

We ended up on a double date. My dad, who's a charmer just like Jay, told me early on, "This is the one."

Jay's proposal went like this: "I'd just as soon marry you as have you move to Colorado." Quote, unquote. But he was nervous—kept rolling the car window up and down.

I asked my stepmom how you know when a guy is the right one. She said, "Sydney, eighteen is young. But you're lucky enough to find early what most girls look for their entire lifetime."

For a good many years it seemed like she was right. Jay and I didn't suffer any period of adjustment. There was no stress. Our families loved each other and we had enough money to go to Friday night parties at the American Legion. I got pregnant at nineteen. Jay was ecstatic.

In retrospect, we started our marriage in a horrible way: living apart. Jay was working in Topeka, Kansas. He'd come home on the weekends. But we lacked everyday togetherness—those little opportunities to truly bond as a couple. He wasn't around to feel the baby kick—or when I gave birth.

I wasn't lonely—I'm not a person who gets lonely—but Jay and I led parallel lives. I didn't realize there were cracks in the marriage until after eight years of marriage when I learned my husband was sleeping with my best friend.

How did I find out? I went to do the laundry and saw strange lipstick on Jay's shirt. I was crushed. We had three toddlers; I had never worked outside the home. Jay did move out for a while. In my heart of hearts I didn't want to divorce. I wanted to discover the reason for the infidelity and how to fix things so it wouldn't happen again.

The marriage counselor saved our relationship. How? By sitting us down together and making us hear the hard facts. He said, "Sydney, no wonder Jay found another woman. You take care of the kids, you mow the lawn, pay the bills, and clean out the garage. I've never known a man that felt less needed than Jay."

He was right. My sister and I had been raised to be independent . . . leaders, not followers. Once the counselor's words sank in I shifted some of the blame for our troubles onto my shoulders.

During this period I cried a lot. I was constantly tired. One night I just lay on the bed, drained, and said, "God, I can't do this anymore. It's in your hands. I want Jay back." I took the deepest sigh, rolled over and went to sleep. It was an unbelievable unburdening. I just didn't worry anymore. I knew Jay and I would make it.

Maybe it sounds like I was weak to forgive my husband for cheating on me. But I feel the opposite is true. My priority was keeping my family together.

For the next three or four years we did things differently and life was absolutely wonderful. I let Jay mow the lawn and take out the garbage. He came home for dinner instead of going out for drinks with the guys.

Gradually we started slipping back into our old personalities. Outwardly, the good times were rolling—ski trips, entertaining Jay's customers, weekends on the boat with the girls. Inwardly, we were back to our parallel lives. I was wrapped up with the girls and Jay with his job. We didn't fight but it was a tense environment. Jay was so hard to live with that my daughter had a dream that her dad opened the refrigerator and got mad because there were no smoked oysters.

I should have picked up on signals. But I was the type who only saw the good in people. One time when Jay was still supposed to be out of town I drove by one of the local establishments and saw his car. I went in. There my husband was, talking and laughing with six guys and girls.

I said, "What are you doing here?"

He answered, "I got back a little early and stopped in here."

This didn't give me pause at all. I said, "I'm on my way to work. See you later. Bye."

While Jay and I were on a cruise I found a receipt for a watch he'd bought another woman. Instantly I was sick to my stomach. When I confronted Jay with this evidence his reaction was denial.

I was angry that he didn't have the balls to tell me there was another woman. He stopped denying the truth but didn't apologize—or swear it would never happen again.

I said, "Why? Do I not keep a clean enough house? Do I not cook good meals? Am I not attractive?"

He replied, "You're a fine woman. You're gorgeous. You keep a wonderful house and cook wonderful meals."

There was no point in trying a counselor again—been there, done that. We both knew it was time for him to leave.

The second he walked out the girls and I bought nail polish (Jay *hates* it!) and sat around painting our fingers and toes.

The last time we'd split I'd gone to Lynn's house, thrown her clothes out the window, and taken pleasure when they landed on the tops of trees. Now I was forty and didn't have the energy to be angry or pull stunts.

There was little animosity. I felt sorry for Jay. He'd given up so much—his home, daily interaction with his children.

The separation was emotionally necessary but financially difficult for both of us. As the years passed the five-bedroom, two-storey house became an anvil around my neck. I didn't invite Jay back out of nostalgia for the marriage. I wanted to keep the family afloat.

Since there was no stress to reconcile we had wonderful times—lots of laughing and hanging out with our daughters. We started having some wonderfully heated and constructive discussions. I said, "How come we couldn't fight like this when we were married?" Another thing we learned was to clean up one problem area at a time. If you try to correct everything all at once, it becomes overwhelming.

After a year Jay said, "Sydney, I'm not gonna go on like this forever. What are we going to do?"

We'd been apart eight years. I hadn't found anyone better. We had these great kids and knew each other's strengths and weaknesses.

Once I said yes, there were no doubts. I knew that Jay would never cheat again. He was aware there were consequences to his actions.

This is not the same marriage as our last two. It's third-time lucky. When we first met, I thought Jay hung the moon and the stars. This time around I know he's intelligent in some areas and stupid in others. I still love him but I'm no longer a pleaser. After we remarried he sat on the couch saying, "Sydney, I'm out of underwear. . . ." I said, "You've been doing your laundry the past eight years. The wedding band isn't changing that."

A friend said to me, "Sydney, you gave Jay too much rope, too much freedom. He lost some respect—that's why it was easy for him to betray you."

That statement taught me that you have to set ground rules and rein in a husband when necessary. I look on Jay's infidelities as his being sick. He was off his rocker. He's well again.

Yes, Jay cheated on me. But in the first two marriages the girls and I cheated on Jay by not making him an integral part of the family. Now we are an indestructible unit that will stay together forever.

Relationships are strong and delicate at the same time. Jay and I live in the moment. Life is too short to get agitated about things that aren't really important. So he's not perfect. Neither am I.

My motto: To live in the past is to rob the present. To forget the past is to rob the future.

Sherry Says

The immediate—and understandable—reaction when faced with evidence that your partner has cheated is to bail on the relationship. However, as Sydney and Jay learned (and subsequently relearned), divorce is not always the best solution to this painful but irrefutably common marital trauma.

Look before you leap out of the marriage: Was the infidelity the latest in a series of callous, abusive acts your partner has committed toward you? Or, was the affair a sign that a cancer exists in the heart of the marriage—a cancer caused by emotional ailments that might or not be curable?

If both spouses are willing to begin the arduous process of rebuilding the marriage (and, of course, the cheater *ends* the affair) rapprochement might be infinitely preferable to the alternative.

Where Jay Erred

This is no modern-day sensitive guy given to fits of self-examination and exhaustive conversations about *feelings*. Rather, Jay is a direct descendent of grunt-uttering cave-men. For years his pattern was to spy what or whom he wanted—and instinctually go after it (thankfully not by clubbing it over the head). Thus he wed Sydney rather than watch her go off to Colorado with her family; did not hesitate to accept an out-of-town job assignment even though his teenage bride was expecting, made partying with work buddies a habit rather than an occasional indulgence, and attributed sleeping with his wife's best friend to *being in the wrong spot at the wrong time*. Having been forgiven once for the sin of adultery, Jay tested his wife's forgiveness capacity by falling off the infidelity wagon a second time.

Finally, on the night before his divorce was final Jay allowed pride, fear, and an inability to clearly communicate his desires keep him from asking his estranged wife for his dearest desire—a reconciliation.

Where Jay Shone

He possessed the capacity to have fun with his family—treating his wife and daughters to weekends aboard a cabin cruiser and to wonderful vacations. After his marriage (take 1) fell apart, he consented to and benefited from marital therapy despite believing the *counselor to be a brick short of a full load*.

Despite the communication breakdown and resultant acrimony between him and Sydney, he never said or did the unforgivable. Even on the eve of breaking up with his wife, he told her: *You're a fine woman. You're gorgeous. You keep a wonderful house and cook wonderful meals*. Postdivorce, he spent lots of quality time with his three children.

It takes a certain kind of man to move back into his family's house as a rent-paying boarder. And a certain kind of man to watch the woman to whom he'd been wed for twenty years leave the house they now shared platonically to go on dates. And it takes a remarkable man to lay his heart on the line and beseech his ex: *If God would answer my prayers, the one thing I'd ask for would be for us to get back together for the rest of our lives*.

Jay has morphed into a millennium-style caveman. He still doesn't enjoy talking about feelings but will do it for the good of his marriage. He has learned to think before acting. Having survived two marital breakups and a heart transplant, Jay will never indulge a momentary whim if it will endanger the thing in his life he now holds most dear: family.

Where Sydney Erred

Sydney's actions are marked on the generation curve, which in 1960 condoned eighteen-year-old girls walking down the aisle. Thus, I won't come down too hard on her following her step-mom's advice and dropping out of junior college to get the coveted M.R.S. degree. She also was too young to be cognizant that the best way to build a strong marriage is to actually live with her bridegroom.

In hindsight, Sydney has realized many of her errors. These include being oblivious that her husband felt excluded by his household of women, not making an effort to communicate with Jay, and allowing him to feel it was a-ok to come home early from a business trip and head to a bar to hang out with women.

By the late 1960s feminism was blooming but Sydney remained locked in the pre-lib dogma which relegated women to the role of homemaker. This belief system drove her to forgive Jay for his virgin infidelity in large part out of fear that she couldn't make it on her own.

It's a shame that after going through all the hard work of revitalizing the marriage, Sydney allowed herself and Jay to sink back into their old dysfunctional ways of non-relating which contributed to the second infidelity and the marriage's demise.

Where Sydney Shone

She is a "glass half-full" person. Her mother's desertion to run off and become a model did not erode Sydney's ability to trust. She transferred her childish affections to *the most wonderful stepmother ever* and retained faith that love and marriage were attainable goals. Once married, Sydney never wavered from the core belief that her primary focus was her family. This belief enabled her to do what needed doing when Jay's first infidelity threatened the bedrock of her life. Yet she was ultimately able to divorce Jay and enter the work world when marriage to a two-time cheater became unendurable.

Sydney's courageous, creative, forgiving spirit is evidenced by her unorthodox offer to her ex-husband: *Come be my boarder so we can save the family homestead.* She would not have agreed to remarry Jay unless she truly felt they both had changed enough to stay happily married for the rest of their lives.

Your Love Lesson From This Couple's Breakup

According to a 1992 survey conducted by the National Opinion Research Center at the University of Chicago, out of 3,432 adults, 25 percent of the men and 17 percent of the women surveyed had been unfaithful. This translates roughly into nineteen million men and twelve million women (one in four spouses!) who have committed adultery.

Although an affair is never justified, if the injured party can come to understand that it occurred because there was something lacking in the marriage, the reasons for the betrayal can become comprehensible, thus opening a window for healing.

Cheating is certainly not a marriage-builder but it needn't be a marriage-breaker.

My Biggest Heartbreak and What It Taught Me About Love

Rene Reid Yarnell, 56, nun-turned-entrepreneur, author of *'Til Death Do Us Part* . . . www.yarnell.com

I've been divorced more than once. The heartbreak is just as agonizing whether it's a college romance that ends, or in my latest case, when the breakup occurs when you are in your early fifties. What does change with age and experience is how you deal with the pain.

My ex-husbands are a former Catholic priest and a former Protestant minister. One marriage lasted seven years; the other for twelve. What helps soften the pain of the losses is that I regard both relationships as key events in helping to shape my life story. There was much good I derived from my time with each of these men. For instance, my second husband gave me the confidence to become a professional speaker and author. I wouldn't have pursued either vocation without his encouragement.

I don't believe that when a relationship ends one partner was more at fault than the other. Wrapping my heart in anger and recriminations would be such a waste. It's not so much about learning from my mistakes as it is about absorbing the best parts of the relationship. There is something extraordinarily special about knowing there is someone out there with whom I shared such a depth of physical and emotional intimacy.

I also believe that important as a love relationship is, there is always life beyond it. When someone important exits center stage, I've learned to take hold of myself and actively create the next phase of my existence. Breakups are not failures, but stepping-stones.

My goal is to leave this world a better place than when I came into it. So nothing makes me happier than when a former husband calls years later and says, "I know we did the right thing to split up, but I want you to know that I'm a better person because of the time I spent with you."

Chapter 22

Making These Love Lessons Stick

It's one thing to be aware that you have negative romantic patterns you continually repeat; another entirely to actually stop those self-defeating behaviors. The good news: With will and work, change is possible. I picked the brains of a variety of leading therapists and experts to provide you with tips that prove an old dog can learn new tricks:

Take a Cue from Gloria Gaynor.

Whether or not there is a partner at your side, *you will survive*. Making it though a breakup without cracking up (at least not permanently) gives you an underbelly of strength. It may not yet be of industrial-strength size proportions but it's a start. To coin another lyric associated with a pop-culture icon, once you emotionally own that *you're gonna make it after all* you no longer need a lover to make you feel whole. Ergo, you no longer need to act in the old self-defeating ways.

Dr. Alma Halbert Bond, Ph.D., author of *I Married Dr. Jekyll and Woke Up Mrs. Hyde or What Happens to Love* (iUniverse.com, 2000), puts it this way, "Many people are afraid to leave bad relationships because these negative love affairs psychologically thrust them back into early childhood. Consequently, they suffer all over again the terror of potentially being separated from a parent. Happily, finding the courage to leave an adult relationship sends the message that you are no longer a helpless child. Finding a partner then becomes the gravy, not the meal."

Guess what? When you maintain such a healthy mindset, that is when love is likeliest to come knocking at your door.

Have a One-Person Pity Party.

Is grief from a failed relationship still holding you a prisoner? Suggests Dr. Kate, author of *Dr. Kate's Love Secrets: Solving the Mysteries of the Love Cycle* (Paper Chase Press, 2000), "Give in to the pain. Tell yourself, 'I will let myself grieve.' Then get out all the pictures of the two of you together and voice all those irrational thoughts like, 'No one will ever love me again.' Keep going until a little voice inside says, 'I don't care.' That's when you should take an aspirin and go to sleep."

Dr. Kate adds, "The next day when you wake up you'll be in a rational state. Repeat this ritual as often as needed. Eventually you will achieve true closure."

Perform a Closure Ritual.

You can't truly move on from the failed relationship until you emotionally lay it to rest. A symbolic gesture can be a start toward accomplishing this goal. One woman, furious after her husband left her for a younger woman, couldn't rid herself of all-consuming anger until she wrote him a letter venting *every* ounce of vitriol in her system. The point wasn't to send the mad missive but to complete unfinished business. She ripped the letter into pieces, flushed it down the toilet, and with that, flushed away a large part of his hold on her.

Pretend You Are Shoe (Not Mate) Shopping.

Dr. Noelle Nelson, author of *Dangerous Relationships: How to Stop Domestic Violence* (Perseus, 2001) says, "Many people devote more effort to buying footwear than to choosing a lover. You don't just box up the shoes and take them home. You try them on, see if they're comfortable, and think how they'll go with the outfits hanging in your closet. If the shoes don't pass these tests, you put them back and let another pair catch your eyes."

The author, whose Web site is *www.dr.noellenelson.com*, continues, "Break the bad habit of getting hooked on someone instantaneously. Instead of mindlessly going with the intense feelings, think about whether he's right for you. Check your prospective partner out in a variety of situations before taking him home. Don't just do a series of dinner and movie dates, go bowling, meet his friends, have him meet yours."

The moral: The blisters that arise from wearing an ill-fitting pair of shoes fade more quickly than the emotional boo-boos you'll suffer from choosing the wrong partner.

Don't Find a Partner Only to Lose Yourself.

It's a familiar scenario. You're an independent, fun-loving, opinionated, intelligent person. Then you fall in love and become what Dr. Gilda Carle calls "a shadow of your partner." The author of *He's Not All That!: How to Attract the Good Guys* (HarperCollins, 2001) and *Don't Bet on the Prince!: How to Have the Man You Want by Betting on Yourself* (Golden Books, 1999), says, "This is a phenomenon that happens mostly to a woman. She loses herself so totally in the guy, that all the traits that originally attracted him no longer exists. How could they when she exists solely to please him? Perhaps she's put on hold plans to go back to school or start a business because he objects." Dr. Carle cautions, "The more you give up for him, the less he appreciates you, and the more likely he'll dump you."

To forestall this destructive cycle starting up again with a new relationship, Dr. Carle suggests, "Remember the *I* part of *I love you*. It's healthy, not egocentric, to consider your needs in a relationship. Also remember how awful it felt to be a slave to the whims of your ex. If you sense warning signs that you're starting down that love junkie road with a new partner, heed these signals instead of ignoring them because it feels so hedonistically wonderful to be in love. The reality is eventually you'll wake up from that passion haze and be miserable. Who needs that?"

Know Thy Patterns.

The key to finding the right person is to *be* the right person. Figuring out just what you've done right and wrong in relationships past will enable you to do better in relationships future. How do you develop that knowledge? Chart out a romantic resume of your love history. After one woman wrote out the details of four failed romances she realized not only that she kept picking men who couldn't commit, but that she wasn't always answering her lovers' needs, either. In two instances, when they'd asked her to do small favors, she'd refused.

By writing out your relationships, you'll clearly see what you got out of them, didn't get out of them and how they affected you. This will help you realize your romantic strengths and also how to overcome your weaknesses.

Know Thyself.

Understanding your romantic patterns is one piece of the puzzle. Another is to understand yourself and what's important to you. Dr. Noelle Nelson explains, "The biggest mistake many of us make is to adopt an image of our ideal mate that's been shaped by the media, our mothers, or our friends. What if, say, you're not career driven and you've been manipulated into seeking out workaholics?"

There is a better way. Explains Brendan Tobin, a personal and professional success coach and author of *Yes You Can: Extraordinary Results From Ordinary People* (Replica Books, 1999), "To find the right mate you need to put pen to paper and develop a plan based on true self-understanding. Once I realized that my pattern was to date women who needed to be rescued, I sat down, admitted to myself the ways I'd contributed to the breakup of those relationships, who I was now (i.e., a guy interested in finding a woman who is strong in her own right) and wrote down the qualities I wanted my next, hopefully, *last* partner to possess. I am now married to my ideal woman."

Divorce Yourself from Your Parents' Negative Influence.

Attraction is an esoteric concept. Too often we find ourselves craving or not craving someone because he or she unconsciously triggers memories of our parents. Anne Teachworth, MA, Director of the Gestalt Institute in New Orleans (*www.gestalt-institute.com*) says, "Our parents' method of relating is imprinted on us for better or for worse. But you can rewrite that imprint and change the sort of person you are attracted to."

This sounds like a tall order but Teachworth has a plan. "Let's say that you typically choose members of the opposite sex who are emotionally closed because that's how your dad acted with your mom. Remember a scenario between your parents—perhaps featuring your mother begging him to talk to her, and him refusing. Mentally revise the way the scenario played itself out. On paper write down the revised version that has your dad being expressive and giving. Read this scenario over and over each night like a bedtime story. Create new scenarios starring your new emotionally open dad." Teachworth concludes, "If you do this at least twelve times you will notice a difference in your attraction pattern."

Stop, Erase, Replace.

It takes twenty-one days to change a bad habit regardless of whether that habit is smoking or repeatedly choosing the wrong type of romantic partner. So says Megan Johntz, an LA-based psychotherapist and public speaker. Johntz, whose Web site is *www.meganjohntz.com*, explains, "Research proves that you can literally reform the makeup of your brain in that time frame by creating new neural pathways."

It works like this: When you get the unwanted thought (*I'm only attracted to lounge-lizards who invariably cheat on me. Straight-laced guys are boring*), stop it. This can be accomplished by screaming at yourself, *STOP, STOP, STOP*; visualizing yourself writing the thought on a blackboard, then erasing it; or seeing the intrusive thought on your computer screen, then hitting Ctrl, Alt, Delete. Replace that thought with *I want a true, solid person who will love only me the rest of my life*. Pummel that thought into your head: Write it out 500 times, scribble in on Post-its you attach all around your house, record yourself saying this new belief and play it over and over while you sleep.

Johtz promises, "After you create these new mental patterns, you really will notice a significant change."

Be a Pollyanna.

Keep telling yourself, "All I'll ever meet are losers," and the prediction will prove an accurate one. Before you set out your shingle as a fortune-teller, consider that what you are is not psychic, but victim of a self-fulfilling prophecy. How much happier an outcome you can elicit for yourself if you think positive thoughts . . . and back up those thoughts by implementing some of the positive tips outlined in this chapter.

Stop Thinking of *Mate* as Analogous to *Noose*.

Many singles, much as they moan about not having someone special in their lives, do everything possible to sabotage potential relationships. The reason: Although most want lasting love, they are subconsciously afraid that a partner would cramp their style. According to Irina Harris, a New York psychotherapist, "In some people's minds, settling down means settling. They fear that once coupled, they won't be as open to new, exciting experiences that make them feel fully alive." She adds, "This spontaneous part of their personality curbs itself when another person's point of view becomes relevant. Personal stagnation can then set in."

If the above resonates for you, Harris has some fuel to douse this potent form of commitment-phobia. She suggests, "Ask yourself what opportunities you fear losing out on if you try lasting romance. What are the things you enjoy that don't seem to fit your idea of a couple? What are *you* truly afraid of?"

Brainstorm the answers to these questions and you'll have a roadmap of areas to look at which can allow you to deduce whether you can share these parts of yourself with another person. Harris concludes, "It's safer to take emotional risks with people that are just passing through your life, but ultimately not as rewarding."

Search for Real, Not Reel Love.

So besieged are we by the Hollywood-fueled image of what a healthy relationship should look like, sound like, taste like that it's often difficult to recognize a potential compatible partner. Perhaps time after time you run toward tall, gorgeous men who resemble movie stars. But a short, balding guy can be a real life Romeo if given half the chance. Break out of the box and open your eyes to new possibilities.

Also open your eyes to the possibility that what you seek isn't the traditional marriage and kids fantasy portrayed on TV. Irina Harris says, "If you're career driven, perhaps a long-distance relationship would work best. Don't worry about what the media says or what your friends and family will think. There are many ways to live a life and conduct a relationship. You need to choose the right way for you."

Rx for Intimacy Bolters.

Denver Psychologist Carolyn Bushong has a surefire method for discerning whether the reason your relationships constantly fizzle is not because the right one hasn't come along, but because you're afraid of intimacy. The author of *The Seven Dumbest Relationship Mistakes Smart People Make* (Fawcett, 1997) says, "Think back to the point at which you typically break off a love affair. Is it when things get really intense and /or when issues arise that require a compromise? Intimacy avoiders use this sort of situation as an excuse to bail."

The way to overcome this tendency, according to Bushong, is by forcing yourself to work through the issue at hand with your latest partner. "One of my clients swore she'd never date a smoker. Or if she met one who attracted her, that she'd end things unless he swore to give up nicotine. While we were working together on her intimacy problems, she met a smoker. Rather than issuing an ultimatum, she expressed a willingness to compromise. The upshot: He won't smoke in her car or in her home but when they're out in public, he's free to light up. They will adhere to this policy even after their marriage next month."

Always the Dumpee? Try This.

Bushong says: "The pattern of being rejected, then trying anything and everything to win back your lover is usually rooted in an early incident of feeling abandoned by someone you loved and trusted." She adds, "Think back. Was the rejecter your father, your first love, perhaps even an uncle or teacher who made you feel not quite good enough? Consequently, when you enter relationships where your ego is on the line, that not-quite-good-enough feeling kicks in and makes you say and do desperate things to recapture the love object's affection."

Bushong's remedy to this desperate downward spiral is to confront the person who initially caused you the emotional damage—if possible in person or over the phone. "For instance, tell the ex-boyfriend who left you for a *Playboy* centerfold, then got dumped in turn, that he was wrong to leave. You're a much better person than he deserved in the first place, an infinitely lovable human being."

If you won't or can't do this confrontation in person write a letter as per the closure ritual. Emotionally divorce this person and the bad self-image he or she foisted upon you.

Enjoy Dating for Its Own Sake.

You can't hurry love. Internet relationship advice columnist Kimberly Williams points out that an error made by many women the moment they meet a man, is not that they want to undress him but to clothe him. Specifically in a tux standing by the altar. The man in question will invariably respond to this unspoken but obvious pressure by running for the hills. Williams, who can be reached at *www.aalize.com*, suggests, "Loosen up. Have fun and enjoy the moment."

Until the two of you make a commitment, don't shut yourself off from other options. You are free to meet and date other men. Exercise this privilege rather than tying yourself up in knots over a man who at this early stage of the game is probably out for laughs, not life.

God Gave You Eyes, a Mouth, and Ears. Use Them.

Really see your partner, speak to him/her and *listen* to the response. Many of the couples interviewed for this book were so wrapped up in their individual "stories" that they had little or no idea what was actually going on in their partner's head and heart. Their subconscious decision to stay cocooned in self-delusion rather than face the truth led to years of uneasy matrimony.

Diana had ample clues that Tom was gay but ignored them all rather than acknowledge that her husband, the father of her two children, preferred men. Barry thought his wedding day to Suzanne was the happiest of both their lives; she had spent that afternoon in bed with a lover, then hysterically crying at the thought of her imminent nuptials.

Just Because It's the Opposite Sex Doesn't Mean You Must Be in Opposition.

It's common (though harmful) to hold the view that men and women are alien species with different values and goals. Such a viewpoint plants the seeds for distrust and fear between the sexes. You can best cultivate seeds for a relationship that can flourish by looking at a new partner in your life as an individual, rather than as someone who will hurt you in exactly the same ways as past lovers.

Marriage and family therapist James Koval, who is professor of Family Studies at California State University in Long Beach says, "One of the biggest problems for people getting back out there after a breakup is a lack of trust in the opposite sex. Such a lack of trust can be an *other*-fulfilling prophecy whereby your negative expectations cause the dreaded behavior from your partner that you most fear."

Be Willing to Give Love.

This sounds obvious but many relationships derail because both partners want to be loved while neither wishes to give it. The fear is that if you give love you'll lose something. The reality is that if you're willing to offer another human being the love you secretly crave, it will boomerang back to you.

A relationship shouldn't be a power struggle, but a mutual surrender to the other. The happiest couples know that their individual power is partly due to a willingness to give as well as take.

Distinguish Between *Attachment* and *Love*.

Meditation teacher Sharon Salzberg explains, "The word *love* has many meanings. One of those is attachment, which is based on having expectations that you need the other person to meet. When they're not met, you're devastated."

The author of *Lovingkindness: The Revolutionary Art of Happiness* (Shambhala Publications, 1997) continues, "When you attach to another person you want to control him or her, you don't want things between you to ever change. But that's unrealistic. Life is about change."

Healthy love, according to Salzberg, whose Web site is *www.loving-kindness.org*, is based on a "clear seeing" of the other person. Think of Sydney, who understands Jay inside and out, and accepts him without idealizing him or needing him to satisfy her every need. Attachment happens when you're operating from insecurity and fear; love comes from opening your heart.

How can you detach from the need to attach? Salzberg suggests, "Realize that you've been taught to look outward instead of inward for the source of your happiness. Realize it but don't judge yourself harshly for subsequently clinging to the person you believe can give you the fulfillment you seek. Looking honestly at yourself takes strength and involves pain. But we grow from pain."

Yes, we grow into having the ability to truly love.

Bare Yourself—Emotionally.

The act of opening up and letting someone special, someone you have solid reason to trust, *really* know you is a risk. It requires more courage and heart than any other human endeavor. There is no guarantee that your bravery and vulnerability will be rewarded with a "happily ever after" ending. There is a guarantee that if you guard yourself against love, you will ultimately lose more than you gain. Remember the cast-iron plate Thomas built around his heart that ultimately cost him Stacey? Know that even if the relationship ultimately doesn't last you'll still be the richer for having allowed another person into your life.

Loving and being loved is a journey, not a destination. I hope this book has served as your boarding ticket.

Bibliography

Books

Generation Ex: Tales from the Second Wives' Front by Karen Karbo (Bloomsbury Pub., 2001). Offers frank and funny advice to help exes cope with the aftermath of divorce and the resultant changes in the family structure.

Spiritual Divorce: Divorce as a Catalyst for an Extraordinary Life by Debbie Ford (Harper San Francisco, 2001). Advice on how to transform divorce into a spiritual wake-up call.

Relationship Rescue: A Seven-Step Strategy for Reconnecting with Your Partner by Phillip C. McGraw, Ph.D. (Hyperion, 2000). Dr. Phil helps estranged couples work through their problems. Also, *The Relationship Rescue Workbook* by Dr. Phillip C. McGraw, Ph.D. (Hyperion, 2000).

Exorcising Your Ex: How to Get Rid of the Demons of Relationships Past by Elizabeth Kuster (Fireside, 1996). A hilarious compendium of real life tricks used by the spurned to stop pining over the one that got away.

Don't Call That Man: A Survival Guide to Letting Go by Rhonda Find-ling (Hyperion, 1999). Includes exercises and trenchant tips aimed at helping the reader let go of an ex and move on.

Heal Your Heartbreak: How to Live and Love Again by Charles Spezzano (Marlowe & Company, 2001). Based on the author's twenty-eight years of counseling experience, this book has lots of practical wisdom to help readers take back their personal power.

Coming Apart: Why Relationships End and How to Live Through the Ending of Yours by Daphne Rose Kingma (Crest, 1989). The author demonstrates how you can use the breakup to become stronger and more able to love.

Uncoupling: Turning Points in Intimate Relationships by Diane Vaughan (Vintage, 1990). This well-researched book explains in lucid and engaging detail the turning points in intimate relationships showing that there are basic similar patterns.

After the Breakup: Women Sort Through the Rubble and Rebuild Lives of New Possibilities by Angela Watrous and Carole Honeychurch (New Harbinger, 1999). The authors, both breakup survivors, gathered the stories of other women whose long-term relationships had ended. The result is inspirational and helpful.

Looking for a Fight: A Memoir by Lynn Snowden Pickett (Dell, 2000). After an emotionally bruising divorce the veteran journalist took up boxing to release some of her aggression. She found what she was looking for . . . and then some.

Falling: The Story of One Marriage by John Taylor (Ballantine, 2000). The author, an ex-*Esquire* writer, says, "Marriage doesn't just break down."

I Married Dr. Jekyll and Woke Up Mrs. Hyde or What Happens to Love by Dr. Alma Halbert Bond, Ph.D. (iUniverse, 2000). Based on interviews with seventy-one divorced women, the author comes up with solutions to end what she calls "the divorce plague."

The Seven Dumbest Mistakes Smart People Make by Carolyn Bushong (Fawcett, 1997). Through real-life case studies, clear explanations, and proven advice, Bushong challenges readers to take control of their love lives.

If the Buddha Dated: A Handbook for Finding Love on a Spiritual Path by Charlotte Kasl, Ph.D. (Penguin, 1999). In this playful yet practical guide, Kasl shows you what it would be like to have the ancient wisdom of the Buddha to guide you through the dating process.

Yes You Can: Extraordinary Results From Ordinary People by Brendan Tobin (Replica Books, 1999). This book is designed as a launching pad to get you back on the path toward your goals and dreams!

Dr. Kate's Love Secrets: Solving the Mysteries of the Love Cycle by Dr. Kate Wachs (Paper Chase Press, 2000). Dr. Kate's concept of the Love Cycle—a series of relationship stages we go in and out of over our lifetime— makes for fascinating reading.

Dangerous Relationships: How to Stop Domestic Violence Before It Stops You by Dr. Noelle Nelson (Perseus, 2001). An important book for every woman who has had an abusive relationship, or who is newly in to a relationship in which there are warning signs surrounding control and power.

'Til Death Do Us Part . . . by Rene Reid Yarnell (Quantum Leap, 2001). Yarnell's focus is on raising consciousness that what is needed postbreakup is less focus on blame and guilt and more appreciation for the shared love and personal growth that was experienced while together.

Don't Bet on the Prince!: How to Have the Man You Want By Betting on Yourself by Dr. Gilda Carle (Golden Books Publishing Company, 1999). A guide to helping women become stronger and more independent.

Practical Intuition in Love: Let Your Intuition Guide You to the Love of Your Life by Laura Day (Harperperennial Library, 2000). Exercises that can help steer you to the love of your life. Also *The Circle: How the Power of a Single Wish Can Change Your Life* (Jeremy Tarcher, 2001).

Getting the Love You Want: A Guide for Couples by Harville Hendrix, Ph.D., (Harperperennial Library, 1990). Troubled couples have found this book recounting Hendrix's program life-changing.

Lovingkindness: The Revolutionary Art of Happiness by Sharon Salzberg (Shambhala Publications, 1997). The founder of the Insight Meditation Society in Massachusetts focuses on a Buddhist practice that emphasizes feelings of love, happiness and compassion.

Online

www.divorcemagazine.com. An extensive resource encompassing legal, financial, and emotional ramifications of divorce.

www.aalize.com. Internet advice columnist Kimberly Williams offers advice with attitude.

www.breakupgirl.com. The lighter side of breaking up.

www.iVillage.com. Head to the Relationships channel for my dating column and more.

About the Author

Sherry Amatenstein is the author of *The Q & A Dating Book: Answers to the Thorniest, Sexiest, Most Intimate and Revealing Questions About Love, Sex, and Romantic Relationships.* She is the dating columnist for iVillage.com, conducts dating seminars around the country, personal telephone coaching, and has appeared on numerous talk shows as a relationships expert. Her Web site is luvlessons.com.